QUARTET

QUARTET

a profile of
the Guarneri Quartet

Helen Drees Ruttencutter

LIPPINCOTT & CROWELL PUBLISHERS
New York

Much of the material in this book appeared originally in *The New Yorker* in somewhat different form.

QUARTET. Copyright © 1980 by Helen Drees Ruttencutter. All rights reserved. Printed in the United States of America. No part of this book may be used or reproduced in any manner whatsoever without written permission except in the case of brief quotations embodied in critical articles and reviews. For information address Lippincott & Crowell, Publishers, Inc., 10 East 53rd Street, New York, N.Y. 10022. Published simultaneously in Canada by Fitzhenry & Whiteside Limited, Toronto.

FIRST EDITION

Designer: Ruth Bornschlegel

Library of Congress Cataloging in Publication Data

Ruttencutter, Helen Drees.
  Quartet: a profile of the Guarneri Quartet.
  1. Guarneri Quartet. I. Title.
ML398.G83 785'.0627471 80-7882
ISBN 0-690-01944-0

80 81 82 83 84 10 9 8 7 6 5 4 3 2 1

FOR ARNOLD DOLIN

PART I

On a sunny Tuesday morning in May, the Guarneri Quartet, the preeminent string quartet in the world today, rehearsed at the suburban home of John Dalley, the second violinist, in Haworth, New Jersey. The other members of the quartet live in Manhattan, and according to their custom, the cellist, David Soyer, drove them out. Soyer, who was wearing a sweatshirt and slacks, is a tall, broad-shouldered man in his mid-fifties, with a high forehead, gray wavy hair combed back, blue-gray eyes, an aquiline nose, and an open, affable manner. He wears glasses onstage—the only one in the quartet who does—and he sometimes looks stern, dour. To his amusement, he has often been described by friends as "avuncular," and he could be everybody's favorite professor.

Soyer walked at a fast pace the two blocks to the garage on the West Side where he keeps his red Volvo, carrying his cello in its hard case as if it were weightless, although it is thirty awkward pounds and on tour he will take a cab a few blocks to spare his arm. He commented on the lovely weather to the garage attendant before he put his cello in the back seat and headed up Broadway to Eighty-sixth Street, where Michael Tree, the violist—who had taken a crosstown bus from his home, on the East Side—was waiting on a bench. Tree, wearing a crisp checked sports shirt and slacks, is, at forty-five, the next oldest in the group. He is a trim, handsome man of medium height, with curling brown hair that is thinning on top, a beard and mustache tinged with gold, high cheekbones, and amazing blue eyes that, along with a characteristic blush, seem to register his feelings immediately. He got into the back seat, rested the top of the cello on his lap, and leaned his viola against his knees.

Tree and Soyer both appeared sleepy, but their spirits were high. The end of their 1976–77 season was in sight, and so were the two months' vacation the quartet takes every year. Behind them were a hundred or so concerts and about sixty thousand miles of travel throughout the United States, Canada, Mexico, Bermuda, and Europe. Ahead were two concerts at the Ninety-second Street Y.M.–Y.W.H.A., of French and Czech music, which was not in that season's repertoire (postponed because of a labor dispute—the quartet will not cross a picket line); three concerts in Vancouver, with the pianist Peter Serkin; three concerts at the University of South Florida, in Tampa; a concert at Wolf Trap park, in Virginia; one open rehearsal and a concert at the University of Kentucky, in Lexington; and their final performance of the season, at the Caramoor Music Festival, in Westchester.

Soyer made a left turn on Eighty-seventh Street and drove north on Riverside Drive. He waved a thank you to a woman, walking her dog, who observed the traffic light and did not step in front of his car. A sanitation truck made a U-turn, and Soyer shouted out the window, "Illegal! Illegal!" and then muttered, "Political corruption on the lowest level—the worst kind."

Tree said that he'd spent ten hours the day before teaching at the Curtis Institute of Music, in Philadelphia, and his two-year-old daughter, Anna, woke him a number of times during the night. His son, Konrad, now eight, had done the same

4

thing at that age; both clearly wanted to reassure themselves that he was really home. Tree said he'd been tempted to move to a hotel, but with his luck, "there'd be a brawl going on in the next room and I wouldn't get any sleep anyway."

Arnold Steinhardt, the first violinist, in jeans and a sports shirt, was waiting in front of an apartment building on Riverside Drive. At forty-two, he is the youngest—a thin, tall man (six feet three), who looks even taller because of a thick head of wavy black hair that is just beginning to turn gray. He has a high forehead, heavy black brows that almost meet in the middle, wide-set green eyes, a long nose, a thin mouth. The overall effect is such—especially when he is wearing white tie and tails—that if he were playing in an earlier century, ladies would carry smelling salts in their beaded evening bags. Steinhardt said, "I'm *tired*. I don't want to go to New Jersey. I don't want to rehearse. I resign." Nevertheless, he folded himself into the front seat, violin between his knees, and Soyer proceeded north to the George Washington Bridge.

Tree said that since they'd given themselves a three-day weekend they would have to work from ten to five, instead of their usual ten to one. They planned to rehearse part of next season's repertoire as well as works they would be playing in the immediate future. Soyer said he *had* to quit at one. He had two pupils he didn't want to disappoint. The first, a girl, had learned cello during childhood as therapy for a muscular disease. She had recovered, and she was talented, Soyer said, and so was the other, a boy whose previous teacher's criticism had been savage. Soyer hoped to help bolster the kid's ego as well as teach him to play.

Tree said in that case they should plan a longer rehearsal for the following day. Soyer's talk of pupils reminded Tree of an unnerving experience he'd had at Curtis, where all three men are on the faculty. One of his students—exceptionally talented—had not been working hard enough, and Tree gave him a stern lecture about the need for total dedication in music. To his surprise, the young man began to cry. Tree's eyes widened in astonishment as he talked about it. He seemed stunned. He is a gentle man, and though such scenes are not uncommon between teacher and pupil, it was the first time it had happened to him.

Soyer said, "I used to make my pupils cry, but then I realized they weren't learning anything. They were just crying. So I stopped."

Steinhardt, who had been silent, said, "I had a *terrible* dream last night. I gave a recital and I was so bad that the audience didn't applaud, boo, or hiss. They walked out. I could see their backs; they were silently leaving the hall. Not a sound, and I just stood onstage and watched them leave."

Soyer said, "That's a classic anxiety dream." They drove over the bridge and through a part of New Jersey that is bright with red, pink, and salmon azalea, dogwood, and lilacs in May, and Soyer, who used to live there, rattled off the names of suburbs they were passing through—Englewood Cliffs, Tenafly, Cresskill, Dumont . . . Tree spotted some tennis courts and said wistfully, "Hey, Arnold, look at all those empty courts." Tree and Steinhardt both play tennis, often with each other. Tree said he had a sore right arm and thought it was tennis elbow; he planned to see a tennis pro to find out what he was doing wrong as soon as he had the time.

Soyer said, "I'll give you odds it's not tennis elbow. I bet it's the Schubert. Sasha Schneider told me that every time the Budapest played that piece, the next morning he'd cut himself shaving." The Schubert Soyer referred to was the G Major Quartet—often called the Great G Major by amateurs who play it, because of its length (forty-five minutes, give or take a minute) and the strenuous physical demands it imposes on the performers. The Guarneri had programmed it for the season against the advice of the Amadeus Quartet, who warned them that it was too much to take on tour. The Guarneri offers four different programs each season, and, as Tree explains it, the people who engage them are allowed to choose quartets from different programs: "Like a Chinese menu: one from Column A, one from Column B. And sometimes they don't want anything on the menu. They want a completely different program, and on tour that's hard." The Schubert isn't offered often by other quartets, and the Guarneri sometimes found themselves playing it five times a week. The three lower voices have long tremolo passages—the curse of opera orchestra string sections, which often play nothing else while the entire plot of an opera is outlined for the audience. But pit players can hold back when the wrist and arm grow weary, spell each other to a certain extent. In a quartet, the intensity of each voice must remain constant.

At John Dalley's house, Nancy Dalley was in the kitchen, ironing damp jeans dry for one of the three Dalley children. She is a tall, pretty brown-haired woman, and when Steinhardt walked in, extended his hand, and said, "Hi! I'm Arnold Steinhardt. Could I have some coffee, please?" she laughed, shook his hand, and poured him a cup from a pot she always has waiting for them. She also always has bagels or coffee cake warming in the oven for the coffee break they take midway through a rehearsal.

Dalley was kneeling on the kitchen floor fixing a broken toy. In his early forties, Dalley has a certain look of the Midwest he comes from. He, too, is a handsome man, with brown hair that dips down over his forehead, blue eyes, a slightly upturned nose, and a trim beard. He moves with grace, and the others say there isn't anything he doesn't do naturally with a high degree of excellence. (Steinhardt once said, "John hits a tennis ball and it comes whizzing over the net so fast you don't see it or hear it or believe he hit it.")

Dalley handed the fixed toy to his son, Erik, aged three, and said, "Let's get this over with."

The four went into a small room off the kitchen which barely held them and the stands and four chairs. On tour, they play in some auditoriums with such rotten acoustics—usually multipurpose halls—that they don't care where they rehearse, as long as they can hear each other. They unpacked their instruments, sat down, and tuned. Soyer played a scale and some harmonics on his C string, peeled it off, and said, "A twenty-six-dollar lemon." He replaced it in seconds with a new string he took from his case.

Steinhardt said, "Benny Goodman would like to do the Mozart Clarinet Quintet with us sometime next season. He'll probably want extra rehearsals, but he's fun to play with."

Tree said, "I'd like to do it with Woody Allen," and Dalley rolled his eyes.

Steinhardt practiced a run in the Haydn Opus 77, No. 2 —part of next season's program—and Tree, the quartet's unofficial statistician, said, "Arnold, that quartet has the second-highest note in chamber music, that high D. The highest is in the Mendelssohn Octet—the E-flat."

Soyer, who was waiting patiently, got them to settle down and get to work, as he always does, by saying, "So . . . *Nu?*"

The quartet works hard on new repertoire, rehearsing in the spring and early fall. They want to have each piece firmly and fluidly in their fingers and bow arms, because often on the road their schedule is so tight they're lucky if they have time to even warm up. They have an easy rapport with one another, and it is clear that each respects criticism from the others, and will give a suggestion consideration, even if disagreement is the end result. They pause often to discuss bowings; when two

8

or three or all have the same legato phrase in different voices, or in unison, the bowing should be the same for uniform dynamics. Logically, they begin many phrases with an up bow, at the tip. A phrase often begins quietly and builds in strength. Volume is at the frog of the bow, not the tip. Tree says, "There are many moments when we have to agree on bowings, though I believe we're less rigid than many other groups. We're often playing at different parts of the bow. Oftentimes, in fast writing, in spiccato-type passages, we'll disagree and end up playing what each of us is best at, and we'll attack it from that point of view, hoping to make it sound concerted, rather than stupidly insisting on doing the same thing." Often someone will say, "How are you going to bow that, Arnold?" and as often as not, Steinhardt will say, "What's your pleasure?"

Program notes for Guarneri concerts tell the reader that they are a quartet without a leader. In the days before the Budapest Quartet—in which Alexander (Sasha) Schneider played second violin—the first violin led and the others followed. But it was clear to the Budapest, as it is to the Guarneri, that the classical composers had no such thing in mind. A theme can bounce from one instrument to another like a tennis ball in mixed doubles, and when more than one player has an entrance at the same time, they discuss which one will lead. Sometimes one says he would like the lead, and so it's settled. Quite often there is no debate: the logical choice is Dalley. Tree, who says he is wedded to his pencil, marks everything down. He says he's equally wedded to his eraser, because in the course of polishing a work they often change their minds about earlier decisions.

They discuss diminuendos, ritards, dynamics, at length. They can spend ten minutes arguing about half a bar. Different editions have different editors, and the composer's true

9

intentions are not always known. If no one has seen the auto-graph, the original, there can be a great deal of argument. (At a rehearsal with Peter Serkin of a Brahms piano quartet, Steinhardt could hardly believe the score was accurate; he was the only one instructed to use a mute. Serkin had seen the auto-graph, and said that the viola and cello were originally muted and then the mute marks were crossed out. Steinhardt said, "I bet Brahms didn't cross them out. I bet his maid, Bertha, did.") When editions conflict, the Guarneri do what they feel is most convincing. Steinhardt says, "Someone may feel strongly that a phrase has to have a ritard, or do something of a certain nature, and if there's disagreement he'll take it very much to heart, because it's something he's worked out him-self. After too much argument, you realize that that particular spot is a centimeter long and the whole piece is a hundred *meters,* and it doesn't matter that much. And sometimes when we're split two for and two against a fine point of interpreta-tion, we'll say, 'Let's try it this way tonight and the other way tomorrow.' And then the two who were against find during the performance that it's not so bad after all. These things work themselves out in the playing."

They began the rehearsal with the Schubert E-Flat-Major Opus 125, No. 1—an early work, written when Schubert was still in his teens. It is open, transparent, like some early Mo-zart, but more sentimental. Soyer wasn't enthusiastic about it, and occasionally, as they made their way through it, he'd say, "Aw, Arnold." Steinhardt said, "It's *so* beautiful. Hang in there—you'll grow to love it."

Although Schubert died at thirty-one, his contribution to chamber-music literature is considered by many to be second only to that of Beethoven. In addition to his famous "Trout" Quintet—violin, viola, cello, piano, and string bass—Schubert wrote a string quintet (the C Major, Opus 163) that employs an extra cello, rather than an extra viola, and it has been proclaimed the greatest chamber work ever written. Musicians often say of a piece that touches them deeply that they would like to have that particular work played at their funeral. A prominent English violinist had inscribed on his tombstone the first six-bar theme of the Schubert cello quintet followed by a quote from Shakespeare: "So long as men can breathe, or eyes can see,/ So long lives this, and this gives life to thee." The pianist Arthur Rubinstein has requested that the slow movement be played at his funeral. Sometimes the Guarneri programs it when a cellist they like is in the area. One year when they were on tour in California, they did it, in Palo Alto, at Stanford, with Bonnie Hampton, the cellist in the Francesco Trio, whose playing they knew from the Casals Festival, and the following spring they would do it again, by special request, in New York, with Jules Eskin, the principal cellist of the Boston Symphony.

For the Haydn Opus 77, No. 2, a late work and one of his finest quartets, Dalley produced a score, which he placed on the floor next to his chair. Haydn is considered the father of the string quartet—Mozart dedicated six of his best to him. As many as eighty-three of them can be ascribed to Haydn, if you count, as some musicologists do, "The Seven Last Words of Christ" as seven, rather than one (each consists of one long movement, instead of the traditional four), and include No. 83, which he never finished. After the second movement, the Minuet, the composer stopped. On the bottom of the score, he wrote, *"Hin ist alle meine Kraft, alt und schwach bin ich"*— "Fled is all my strength, old and weak am I." Soyer points out that Haydn lived on for six years. Soyer also says, "Before Haydn sat down to work, he would put on his best suit and his best wig, because he felt that while he was composing he was in the presence of God."

As they made their way through the four movements of the Haydn, they spoke in a kind of shorthand to each other. Points were raised and sometimes not settled. Questions sometimes went unanswered. Dalley said, "I think that ritard is a little obvious," and Steinhardt suggested, "Maybe if we do it but pretend we're not, we can get away with it." Dalley added, "The whole first movement sounds punched, and where did you get that subito piano?" Steinhardt admitted, "It's not in the part. I just made it up." Tree said, "You guys still don't agree on the length of those eighth notes," and Soyer interjected, "They should be *crisp*. Tuck-a-tuck-a-tuck— *not* duck-a-duck-a-duck." Dalley said, "We don't agree on intonation, either. It's hideously out of tune." Soyer added, "We're going to have to make this *move,* or it will get very boring. Can't we play the second part with a little more motion?" At one point, Dalley had the theme, and Steinhardt said, "We're all too loud. John can't be heard. And, John, are you going to make a crescendo there?" Dalley said, "I'm not going to make a big thing of it. It shouldn't sound heavy-handed." Steinhardt complained to Soyer and Tree, "You guys are killing me when I take over the theme from John. Just because you have a forte, you don't *have* to do it. What's marked in the score isn't the last word—it's not the Bible."

Sometimes they continued to play while they talked. Soyer asked, "What will I do with my tonic resolution if you go triple piano there?" And Steinhardt quipped, "I'm sure you'll think of something." Tree said, "Even if the music had no markings, we would instinctively make a crescendo there," and Dalley, ever avoiding the obvious, said, "That's precisely why I don't want to do it." Soyer said, "We're getting impaled on this. Let's back off and approach again."

The slow movement, perhaps reminiscent to them of Haydn's "Emperor" Quartet, whose Adagio is the German national anthem, got them off the musical track and talking in metaphors: "I see shiny helmets, men marching." "Guns and bayonets and tanks are coming." "Soldiers in uniform—thousands of them." "*Sieg heil!*"

The four often talk about a composer as if he were a close friend, and it is not unusual for them to become wildly irreverent while they read through a work they actually revere. Thus, one time when they were working on a Bartók, Soyer intoned as they played, "János has just come home from the war. It is raining, and he is soaked. He falls in the mud, and a pig bites him. The villagers recognize him and they kick him." Bartók went up into the mountains to record peasant folk tunes that he would later incorporate into his compositions, and Steinhardt interrupted Soyer to say, "The peasants were superstitious; they were afraid that if they sang into a tape recorder they would lose their voices, so Bartók hid the mike in a pot of chicken paprikash and said, 'Won't you sing a little tune into my chicken paprikash?' " At this point, they'd stopped playing and were laughing.

Another time, they were rehearsing the Dvořák Piano Quintet with Garrick Ohlsson. In the last movement, the strings play sustained whole notes—an accompaniment to the piano which sounds like organ chords. Soyer said, "He wrote this in a cathedral." The voices part and grow lively, and Tree said, "Now he's in a café, *looking* at the cathedral." Then the string parts become almost raucous, and Steinhardt added, "He's still in that café, but now he's looking at a cathouse."

They ended the rehearsal with a work by the Polish composer Witold Lutoslawski. It is a comparatively modern work, written in 1964. They programmed the piece because they thought it was a good one, and not because of criticism by sponsors that audiences were being "Beethovened to death." Tree says, "We're certainly not the darlings of young composers, though we feel a responsibility as performers to play their works. We play twentieth-century classics—the important works of Schoenberg, Berg, Webern, Stravinsky, Hindemith; but that wouldn't placate most young composers today. They consider the Lutoslawski old hat. We have a closetful of manuscripts, and we read through many of them, but when we program a work it can't be a one-shot thing. We've played Kirchner, the Sessions Second, and taken them into places where the audiences have never heard an American quartet. We'll play a work sixty or seventy or eighty times, depending on how often it is chosen, and we feel we're doing more of a service to modern composers than those who do something once for an audience of intellectuals. We play something new if we think it's good."

As Dalley explained the Lutoslawski, "There are bars, but not always in the same place for each instrument, and instructions. If you follow the viola, say, you can start almost immediately or you can wait awhile; it's up to the individual player. So everything is in a different place within a given framework. The composer doesn't want it played the same way twice, and it's written in a way that makes uniformity impossible. He wants *you* to discover where your notes are in relation to the others'. There are meeting points, marked with letters, and there the bar lines are in the same place. It's like a code. Once you've cracked it, it's tremendous fun to play." The piece begins with the first violin playing an almost inaudible three-note figure, and directions in the part say that the figure should be repeated "until you see the audience has become completely quiet." An unreasonable request, many audiences might feel. This morning, the four were reading through the piece—two movements—together for the first time, and at one point Tree said to Soyer, "Don't worry about losing me.

I know what you're doing at N and I'll catch up with you there."

They'd all been tired at the beginning of the rehearsal, but music seems to engender energy in performers, and when they finished rehearsing they were absolutely hopping.

~

There is an exuberance of chamber music in America today—about two hundred and fifty professional string quartets (and more forming), as opposed to a dozen or so twenty-five years ago, according to Benjamin Dunham, the executive director of a newly founded organization called Chamber Music America. Chamber music has its origins in Europe, where centuries ago only the privileged were educated to understand it, and in many cases perform it. Music commissioned by kings, counts, and princes gradually made its way out of the castles and into concert halls and homes, and it proliferated in Europe. Music has always been written "to order," commissioned to fulfill a need, celebrate an occasion, or utilize specific instruments, but whereas the combinations of chamber ensembles are almost innumerable, the repertoire that has established itself in the past two centuries would indicate that the string quartet—two violins, a viola, and a cello —provided the form many composers found most challenging. The quartet also provides a base for, among other things, piano quintets (quartet plus piano), viola quintets (quartet plus viola), sextets (quartet plus viola and cello), and octets (two quartets). The quartet is also often linked, in various combinations, with the flute, French horn, clarinet, and guitar.

The growth of chamber music in America has been gradual, and, as is true of many art forms here, the reason was partly money—or a lack of it. Many European countries have been generous with groups that perform chamber music, but America has not been. The National Endowment for the Arts allocates funds for musical organizations with budgets of more than a hundred thousand dollars; the line was drawn there to exclude chamber groups, on the ground that there would be no accurate way of gauging the need and quality of such a vast assortment. Chamber Music America was organized in part to help small groups get funding, and it appealed for support to a House subcommittee that deals with the Department of the Interior and related agencies. The appeal, sandwiched between a proposal involving forestry and one on the subject of air pollution, was being considered a part of a general program for improving life in America.

Chamber Music America's appeal did not go unheeded. In 1979 and 1980, the National Endowment for the Arts, working with the National Council on the Arts (a presidentially appointed body made up of twenty-six citizens recognized for their expertise or interest in the arts) apportioned two hundred and fifty thousand dollars each year to a pilot program for small ensemble groups. Based on the success of this pilot program and with the active endorsement of Ezra Laderman, the new director of the NEA's music program, federal funding, supplemented by help from the Ford Foundation, gave a five-hundred-thousand-dollar transfusion to chamber music in America for the 1980–81 season.

~

Thirty years older than Chamber Music America, and possibly a more accurate gauge of the interest in string quartets, is the Amateur Chamber Music Players, Inc., which lists more than five thousand musician members in this country, and about fifteen hundred in sixty foreign countries. Though the ACMP biennial directory includes a variety of instruments—

the saxophone, the trombone, the clarinet—its members are predominantly string players interested only in quartets. Members' addresses and phone numbers are listed, and where they can be reached in the summer, should they be away for any length of time. This indicates a willingness—an eagerness, actually—to be called by anyone anytime to be part of a quartet session. If—heaven forbid—a violist, say, should cancel at the last minute, the directory is invaluable for the three others, who must forgo an evening of musicmaking unless a last-minute sub can be found.

ACMP members rank themselves in an application that includes a questionnaire designed to measure degree of expertise. The form includes questions on the repertoire the applicant can handle: early Haydn, late Haydn, Mozart, Opus 18 Beethoven, middle Beethoven, Brahms, Schubert, late Beethoven, Bartók. Applicants thus place themselves on a scale of A through D, and if a future member is truthful about his ability to play middle and late Beethoven with competence and musicality, he probably deserves to be ranked A, which means excellent and which, in the directory, will follow his name and precede his phone number. The founder and guiding spirit of the ACMP, the late Helen Rice, was a gentle woman who believed all amateur musicians should be encouraged to play, and the other categories are: B—good; C—fair; D—etc. The word "bad" was not in her vocabulary. There is also a Professional category, which includes teachers, retired professionals, and some fringe musicians, such as a retired bandleader who owns a Strad and is prouder of the chamber music he plays than he is of his popular-music career (a radio-show band). If the system has a flaw, it is that there is often a battle over which violinist gets to play first. To the dismay of the violist and cellist, the winner is not always the best. Sometimes the question is settled on a first-to-arrive basis;

sometimes on which has the most chutzpa. Since the first part is more exposed and, in the sheer number of notes to be played, more difficult, an evening with a floundering first is not much fun for the others. The bandleader likes to play first, and since he is not an A player, he usually hires a professional to play cello and coach and keep things on an even keel.

Some members are leery of players who list themselves as A. Often they turn out not to be the best judges of their own abilities, and have less insight into what is involved in playing quartets than a more modest B. And many players are not listed in the directory at all. These are the musicians who, over the years, have made their own connections and don't want to waste an evening with a stranger who might turn out to be a disaster. (One New York violinist who had no reason to think of himself as a disaster took his violin to Paris, on vacation, and arranged a quartet session with an ACMP member there who was willing to host a session. Such willing souls are easy to spot in the directory: their names are preceded by an asterisk. The New York violinist found himself playing in a quartet that included a woman violinist who had won first prize at the Paris Conservatory and was about to leave for Moscow to study with the late David Oistrakh. She played first, of course, and throughout the evening she complained that he was playing too loud. He is fluent in French, and at the end of the evening, packing up his instrument to return to his hotel, he meant to say, *"C'etait un honneur de jouer avec vous."* Instead, he blurted out, *"C'etait une horreur de jouer avec vous."* Another amateur took the QE2 to Europe, and instead of playing shuffleboard or bridge, he practiced his violin most of the day. He felt complimented that no one complained, though it is possible, depending on where his cabin was in the bulkhead, that no one heard him.)

Sometimes four amateurs play together and discover they have a special camaraderie and are also balanced technically. They will play together on a weekly basis for years. Often they engage a professional to coach them; often the music they make is much more than just presentable; and always they have a whale of a good time. (One book on Transcendental Meditation, in an aside, said that people who play string quartets have no need of TM, or, presumably, a mantra.) Vast numbers of mothers who wanted their sons to become another Heifetz had to settle for a doctor or a physicist or a lawyer. (Einstein was an avid and terrible violinist; possibly because of his prestige, Abe Fortas plays violin in quartets with Isaac Stern.) Many members of the ACMP are doctors, and a not surprising number of these are psychiatrists.

As a result of this tidal wave of serious amateur musicians, a number of hotels and motels in resort areas have got a new lease on life by opening their doors to musicians: they offer a special package deal that includes a room and meals; a guarantee of an abundance of musicians to make music with; a library of chamber-music scores; and often a good coach. And all over the country, between the summer and fall sessions, college campuses, and sometimes ski resorts as well (Snowbird, in Utah, for example), are turned over to chamber-music players.

Amateur musicians are indomitable. The 1952 ACMP listed a cellist in Saigon willing to arrange quartets for anyone who might be interested. Not so farfetched. In 1945, a sailor stationed on the Aleutian island Adak was walking down a dirt road the day before a spit-polish inspection. A jeep carrying the base commandant skidded to a halt and the commandant said, "Sailor, you better get a haircut or a violin." The sailor said he *had* a violin, and the commandant had his driver take them both to the sailor's Quonset hut for proof. The sailor played for the commandant, and did not have to get a haircut. (He wasn't the average amateur, though. After the war he went to Juilliard, and he is now a violist in the New York Philharmonic.)

Amateurs are not only indomitable; they are intrepid. The ACMP sends a monthly newsletter to its members, filled with chatty items about what is going on in the chamber-music world and letters received from far-off countries. One horn player wrote that at the height of a small-scale war in Beirut he still managed to play horn quartets with three colleagues almost nightly. The November 1978 newsletter included a brief item headed "Russia: Would You Like to Go There?" It explained that the ACMP had been in close touch with the Citizen Exchange Corps for some time, and under discussion was the plan to let amateur musicians, carrying their instruments, go to Russia. Two Russian experts who were consulted took a dim view of the project; they felt the chances of amateurs from other countries being allowed to play in Russia, except in public buildings, were slim.

Nevertheless, in the spring of 1979, fifteen Americans and one Canadian did make the trip. The November newsletter of that year included a report on the tour: According to John Loud, of Texas, one of the group's leaders, they went to concerts, operas, and ballet, but the musicians they met were either students aiming for a career or established professionals. They even had difficulty translating the word "amateur," which in Russian apparently means "folk music." "The fact is," Loud reported, "they have no single simple term for amateur chamber music, because it is foreign to them." Loud, through the group's interpreter, spoke to one Russian who said, "If our string players as children show enough talent to play classical music, they go the full route and become professionals. Otherwise, they get shunted into the factory folk ensembles. There are not enough instruments to go around anyway." Undeterred, the Western musicians, forgoing a lot of sightseeing, played in hotel rooms, and once, courtesy of their guide, they played in the Kadriorg Palace Museum, in Tallinn. The guide explained to the museum director that Americans had a strange habit of playing just for themselves, and not for an audience, but they wouldn't mind if visitors to the museum paused to listen. The musicians broke up into small groups and played in different rooms; Loud described the experience in his report: "Playing in the Palace in its beautiful 18th century park, its large windows and balconies revealing lawns and flower gardens, the June morning sun pouring in; panelled walls, sculpture and paintings. What more could one ask? But we were still playing with each other."

~

Music is nearly impossible to describe, and few critics capture the beauty and pure joy to be found in it. It often seems that a critic is hell-bent on finding a flaw in a performance—preferably a number of them. It is an unusual review of a good, even great, performance that doesn't include a "however," which is sometimes the strongest word in the review. It is often easy to imagine a critic of a different event, in a different arena, watching a renowned aerialist plunge to his death and saying to himself, "Clumsy, clumsy . . ." So it is possible that amateurs are the luckiest musicians of all, and certainly a key to the abundant joy to be found in it. Most of them would probably rather play than eat, and if their technique falls short of the demands, their imaginations supply what is missing. The literature is unsurpassed in quantity and quality. Occasionally an evening goes so well—on-target intonation with skin-tingling overtones, an absence of dissension, a wonderful rapport with one another, new insights into a quartet they have been playing for years—that euphoria will keep them awake well into the night and they will remember the evening the rest of their lives.

Next to playing, amateurs like to go hear the pros. They often appear at concerts with their instruments—on their way to or from a session. When the Guarneri appeared on the scene, some amateurs were stunned, and some were stung. One especially good amateur violinist dug pretty deep in his search for flaws in the group, and it was several years before he came around to admitting, somewhat abashedly, that they were "the greatest."

~

One of the first prominent American quartets was a wealthy man's plaything, the Flonzaley Quartet—four Europeans indentured in 1903 by Edward J. de Coppet, of New York, and named for his summer estate near Lake Geneva, in Switzerland. The quartet practiced and performed privately for de Coppet for a year before touring Europe and America. De Coppet knew how to keep a quartet together. A clause in the contract the four men signed stipulated that none of them could get married for ten years. They all had mistresses, and when the ten years were up, one of the men said, "There goes my only excuse." (De Coppet had a high regard for music and a low regard for women: In his New York townhouse, one floor was used for quartet concerts. The room was divided by a glass partition to separate the men from the women, on the grounds that the women were bound to chatter and giggle during a concert and ruin it for the men.)

In America in the late fifties, there were two major quartets—the Juilliard and the Budapest. The Budapest, a European group that had settled in America, was the preeminent tet in the world at the time. Philanthropist and music-lover Elizabeth Sprague Coolidge had a special interest in string quartets. She provided funds for a dozen communities across the country to start their own chamber-music series, with the proviso that one modern work be played at each concert. Some unendowed communities, with ongoing chamber-music series, who wanted to engage the Budapest but couldn't afford the fee could get them for less, Mrs. Coolidge making up the difference. But this hurt other quartets. A sponsor was apt to say, "Why should we pay four hundred for the Fine Arts when we can get the Budapest for the same amount?"

Some of the two hundred and fifty professional quartets active today are quartets-in-residence in colleges and conservatories that two decades ago had none. Chamber-music audiences here, at one time predominantly and visibly European, expanded as more and more Americans developed a taste for the music. Over the years, a demand grew that needed a supply. Music-lovers were annoyed by the battering loud sounds that assaulted them everywhere—in elevators, supermarkets, parks, and on some movie soundtracks—and some were getting bored with the steady diet of standard orchestral repertoire and solo piano and violin works. Those who began going to quartet concerts enjoyed the intimacy and interplay of four musicians working together, and even felt included in the performance. In music, familiarity breeds enjoyment if the music is good, and if the government was not providing funds, some individuals and private foundations were—especially after a ruling by the Internal Revenue Service in the nineteen-twenties that music was educational as well as entertaining, that it improved the quality of life in America, and that money donated to further its cause was tax deductible.

Money was, and is, by no means the only major problem. It's always hard for a quartet, for emotional reasons, to stick together. The music they play demands unusual maturity—there is a built-in competition between the two violins—and too often evokes volatile, childish tantrums, as a James Stevenson cartoon some years ago suggested: Four men are sitting in a rubble of broken music stands, scattered music, smashed instruments—the first violinist is wearing the cello like a ruff, and the neck of the viola is dangling by one string. In the caption, the violist is saying, "As far as I'm concerned, gentlemen, this marks the end of the Schwarzwälder String Quartet." There are no records of how many American quartets formed and dissolved like snowflakes or went off like rockets because of lack of success or dissension, or a combination of both.

As the name Flonzaley might indicate, quartet names are chosen from a variety of sources. Some, mostly European, have been named for composers: the Bartók, the Smetana, the Borodin. Some, again mostly European, have been named for the first violinist and let you know who's in charge: the Végh, the Roth, the Kneisel, and the Busch. (The principle of follow-the-leader was carried to extremes by Joseph Joachim, who stood while the others sat. Some older music lovers recall hearing a quartet that billed itself as "Mischa Elman and His Band.") Quartets have been named for countries: the Quartetto Italiano, the Hungarian (two of them), and, holding on to the tail of a kite, the New Hungarian. Some have been named for cities: the Budapest, the Tokyo, and the Hollywood —the last a good quartet which thrived in spite of its name. Some picked names seemingly at random: the Amadeus (Mozart's middle name), the Emerson, the Audubon, the Vermeer. There have been a number of American Quartets and New York Quartets, and now there is one of each, both so good that possibly they're here to stay. They have received high praise wherever they've played, though it took a while before they settled down. The New York—four Juilliard graduates—is in residence at the University of California at Irvine, and the American is at the Peabody Conservatory of Music in Baltimore. Both are quite new, and in the process of settling down they played a game of musical chairs. The second violinist of the New York quit; the violist replaced him, and the violist in the American moved over to the New York. Some quartets have been named for schools: the Manhattan, the Yale, the Curtis, the Cleveland, and the Juilliard, and some for mere proximity to a school, perhaps with the hope that it might help: the LaSalle, for the cross street that bordered the old Juilliard School, at 125th and Broadway. That quartet fared better than the Claremont, named for the avenue that passed Juilliard on its western side, and the Claremont did better than the Tiemann, named for the cross street a block north of LaSalle. Some chose areas famous for instruments made there, and several years ago there were three Cremonas. Some chose instruments' names, even if they didn't own or play them: the Alard (for the Alard Stradivarius), the Stradivari, and the Guarneri. And one quartet—nameless here —composed of first-desk men from a major symphony orchestra, demonstrated how difficult the art is. A critic said of its debut concert: "A string quartet is like a new-born baby. It often comes out wrinkled and ugly, and it will be some time before anyone will know what it's really like."

For a number of years, the Guarneri Quartet was America's, and perhaps the world's, youngest major quartet. There have been changes of personnel in the Juilliard, and of the original four only Robert Mann, the first violinist, remains. Over the years, members of the Juilliard, at Juilliard, coached a number of the current quartets, including the Tokyo, the American, the Concord, the Emerson, and the New World. The most recent additions to the Juilliard have resulted in the average age of that quartet—incongruously celebrating its thirty-fifth anniversary in 1980—being lower than the average age of the Guarneri.

So the Guarneri, in its sixteenth year and with no change of personnel, is now the senior American quartet. They are said to have done for quartet music in America what Leonard Bernstein did for symphonic music—made it accessible and appealing to everyone open to a new music experience. Audiences get a quadruple dose of what many managers consider one of the most important elements for a career in music: charisma. They have been hailed all over the world as "the Great American Quartet of the era" and "the greatest string quartet in the world." According to Harold Schonberg, in *The New York Times,* "It has no superior on the world's stages." In over fifteen hundred concerts, they have postponed—but not canceled—a dozen, and four times, when Michael Tree was sick, they played string trios and piano quartets. On those occasions, Steinhardt played viola. The quartet was invited to play at the White House a number of times, but they would have had to postpone a concert, so they refused. When the quartet was only four months old, Arthur Rubinstein chose it to record the major piano quartet and quintet repertoire. Some younger quartets—the Tokyo, the Vermeer, to name two—are doing exceptionally well, but they will have an Everest climb to catch up with the Guarneri. The Guarneri has been nominated for eight Grammy awards, and its recording of the Cavatina movement from the Beethoven Opus 130 was reportedly encapsulated in Voyager II and launched, possibly into eternity, on August 20, 1977, along with other artifacts chosen to represent the best of American culture.

PART II

Michael Tree's father, Samuel Applebaum, is well known in the music world. He has been on the faculty of the Manhattan School of Music for over twenty-five years, teaching violin. He has written a number of excellent study books on the technique of violin playing that are used in schools throughout the world, and he started his son on violin. The family lived in Newark, and sooner or later all the greats passed through Newark to see Applebaum, and Michael met them. Fritz Kreisler is one of his heroes, and on the piano in the Trees' living room there is a photograph in a silver frame of the great man, with his compassionate face, smiling down at a ten-year-old Michael. Tree is too young to be awestricken, and the two are looking at each other with an openness, a candor that dissolves the sixty-year age gap.

Tree says, "I studied with my father for about eight years, and it worked very well. He broke me in gently and slowly. I never felt I was having a lesson. I had heard fiddle playing in my house from age one, and it was a natural and inevitable part of my life. It would have been amazing had I not become a musician. As is most often the case when fathers teach their sons, it's better that there be a parting of the ways, so when I was twelve I was admitted to the Curtis Institute of Music, in Philadelphia—the only music school I know of that is run totally on a scholarship basis, and, naturally, the caliber of the students there is exceptionally high. Also, I was rubbing shoulders with students almost twice my age, and because they were so good I was bewildered at first."

At Curtis, Tree studied for a year with Leah Luboshutz, a member of the Philadelphia Orchestra, and then with Efrem Zimbalist and Veda Reynolds, each of whom stressed different aspects of violin technique. Zimbalist, Tree says, experimented with new fingerings for the standard repertoire—extending and contracting the hand, using different fingerings, to avoid the traditional position playing and the subsequent and unnecessary shifts. "You have greater elasticity with his approach. It eliminates a great deal of wasted motion. Also, Zimbalist was a concert artist, and he brought concert experiences into the studio. The world of performing has little relationship to what you normally learn in a studio. A good teacher who is also a performer can almost anticipate what will work in a large hall." Tree and Dalley and a Japanese student at Curtis, Toshiya Eto, all spent several summers in Zimbalist's home in Camden, Maine, studying and practicing. Tree remembers it as "a tremendous experience—musically, spiritually, personally."

Tree's career began when he was twenty, with a concert in Carnegie Hall, and he was a success from the start. As Tree, who had changed his name, became well known, people in the music world began quoting his father as saying, "Only Applebaum can make a Tree." Tree went on tour in this country and Europe and South America, giving recitals and playing concertos with a number of orchestras. And in the summer of 1959 he went to Marlboro, a summer music center in Vermont which had been founded in 1951 by Rudolf Serkin, Adolf and Herman Busch, and Marcel, Louis, and Blanche Moyse. The purpose of Marlboro was to provide professionals an opportunity to get together and play all kinds of chamber music—something that would not be available to them in the normal course of their careers. Tree says, "When I first attended Marlboro, I suddenly experienced a new feeling of joy —a happiness about playing. My early experiences there were playing fiddle in pieces like the Schubert Octet, the Beethoven Septet—works with winds—and it was a revelation to me, because I loved the cooperative atmosphere, blending with other players, the exchange of ideas. It gave me much more joy than having to get up and battle against a symphony orchestra—playing triple forte every minute of the time. This may not be publicly understood, but sometimes solo playing is easier. You can indulge yourself in every sort of way. If you're nervous, you take more bows, play a diminuendo here, a slide there—there's much more leeway and much less pressure. There are difficult viola solos in the chamber-music literature that would be a hundred percent easier within the context of a concerto. In an ensemble, you must blend with the others—sometimes imitate another player, continue an idea that's been stated, or a style—and it may be contrary to what you would normally do. I get more frightened in a quartet than I ever do as a soloist."

Of the four men, Tree is perhaps the one most plagued by that musician's nemesis, stage fright. He remembers vividly his first encounter with the ogre. His father held twice-yearly student recitals in the family home, and Tree was eight the first time he was scheduled to perform. He was one of fourteen or so pupils, ranging in age from eight to twenty-two, on the program. He says, "When my turn came, I walked out to play, and suddenly I felt such terror that I turned around and walked right off. I still quake at the memory." However, of the pupils who were on the program that day, Tree is the only one who went on to make a career of music. He feels that stage fright is almost a taboo subject with fellow musicians—something they just don't want to talk about.

Tree had one of his most severe bouts at a Mostly Mozart concert. He recounts, "I was scheduled to play a duo for flute and viola with Jean-Pierre Rampal composed by Franz Hoffmeister, a contemporary of Mozart. I got the music from Jean-Pierre a day or two before the concert, and the first and only rehearsal with him was the day of the concert. There were a million notes in that piece, and at the rehearsal he took it much faster than I'd anticipated. He's not known for his slow tempos. I remember practicing in the living room—with my daughter watching—in an absolute sweat, trying to learn it. I finally said to her, almost imploringly, 'Do you realize that in less than three hours I have to play this for three thousand people, and I still have to learn it? There's no *way* I can get these notes in my fingers between now and eight o'clock tonight.' She looked at me sweetly and said, 'Well, Papa, don't worry. If you can't play the piece, just don't go to the concert.' I've thought about that since. Maybe it's the best musical advice I've ever received."

Tree describes the genesis of the Guarneri: "I met Dave at Marlboro, and the pianist Anton Kuerti, and for a year or so the three of us did quite a few concerts as the Marlboro Trio. Kuerti dropped out, and Mitchell Andrews replaced him. Later, John and Arnold came to Marlboro too, and we had a musical reunion—cemented our friendship. We had been students together at Curtis, and they met Dave at Marlboro. I no longer remember exactly how the quartet was formed. Somebody put a bug in our ear. Sasha Schneider, of the Budapest Quartet, and Rudolf Serkin were very much a part of it. Even Casals was aware of what was going on. At the time, Arnold was the assistant concertmaster of the Cleveland Orchestra, and his contract had a year to go. From our student years, we knew enough about each other's personalities, musical ideas, that we were willing to gamble."

Sasha Schneider, perhaps the most enthusiastic of their mentors, did not consider it a gamble. He says, "Four boys—each a virtuoso, very good musically, and healthy too. My God, it was the most perfect thing. We made it clear that it wouldn't be easy. The most important thing for them, or any quartet, is that after they finish their work they should not be together. And they should not travel together. You are too much together. It is much more difficult than a marriage. In a marriage, there are only two people, and you have to give in to each other—one to the other. With four, it is very difficult, especially if the four have wives. We told them the wives shouldn't mix in at all. They should stay out of things. But the most important thing is that they have the same musical education, the same musical ideas. And each must be strong individually. Four balanced, healthy men. It couldn't fail." (Heaven help the Manhattan Quartet: the two violinists are brothers, the violist and cellist are sisters, and the first violinist and the cellist are married to each other.)

"Basically, we were three violinists and a cellist," Tree has said, "and who played first was decided very quickly." They were quoted in an interview as saying that they drew straws to decide who would play what, but Tree laughs at that. He says, "We were only kidding. We would never do anything that haphazard. We feel each player is equally important—like the four wheels on a car. It's not a comment on John's playing that he's second, or on mine because I'm the violist. When there are two of anything, there are usually numbers attached, but the numbers shouldn't indicate degree of importance." Still, no matter what anyone says, in most quartets there is a tension between first and second that is sometimes insurmountable.

33

Tree says that they agreed in advance that whoever played second would have the option of playing in works that called for only one violin. He adds, "In certain autocratic groups in the past, that would be unheard of. We had all learned viola at Curtis, and I remember wanting to play it in the quartet, never dreaming that we would be quite so busy. I thought of playing viola as something I would do in conjunction with my violin playing. I viewed it as a furthering of my musical experience, not necessarily as a full-time job. But I've come to love it. I think like a violist now. My entire tonal concept has changed. I began to wallow in a much more sensuous, darker, chocolaty sound, and it colored my attitude about music too. I'm not, of course, flying around the fingerboard so much. Viola parts, in general, are not as demanding technically. Also, there is a different way of articulating, because when you're in the middle register, as a violist is, you simply cannot bow and finger things the way you would on the violin and still be heard. You have to emerge. Oftentimes you have to make little accents with both hands—left *and* right—and particularly with little notes, short notes, quick notes. My first glimpse of the realities of playing viola in a group was during our first year, when we played a viola quintet with Boris Kroyt, of the Budapest. He played second, and was seated to my right. Rehearsals went fine, but during the concert, when he had solo notes he wanted to project, I suddenly felt as if he were sitting in my lap. He turned toward the audience, his scroll almost in my elbow, and he managed to project a great deal more—the way a singer does in an opera when he turns and faces the audience. A half turn and the acoustical situation changes."

During the year they waited for Steinhardt to complete his obligations in Cleveland, there was a lot of talk in the music world about the new quartet. Everyone expected it to be spectacular. Tree said, "Mischa told us, 'Don't play a note! You'll ruin your reputation.' We rehearsed when we could in the spring, and in Puerto Rico, during the Casals Festival— every free minute we had—and again at Marlboro, where we played together in public for the first time. The same summer, we gave our first concert on Nantucket, and Harpur College, in Binghamton, a branch of the State University of New York, gave us an in-residence contract at twenty-five hundred apiece for the year. We had very little repertoire, and our backs were against the wall from the beginning. Sometimes offstage we were still rehearsing just before we went out to play—working out last-minute ideas. We had no time to sit around and luxuriate, philosophize, take long months, or even years, as some quartets have done, to develop a style."

Donal Henahan, in the *Times*, in an otherwise favorable notice on a three-year-old quartet, wrote: "It will take a few thousand more rehearsal hours and a few hundred more concert hours, perhaps, but judging from its performances this time the Primavera [four women] could be on its way to take a place among the ranking international quartets." When the Guarneri made their New York debut, in February 1965, the critics had no reservations. And after the concert—in the inauspicious auditorium of the New School, normally not on any critic's beat—Max Wilcox, of RCA, rushed backstage to talk about a recording contract. (Seymour Solomon, from Vanguard, had already approached them, but Wilcox got RCA to top Vanguard's offer.) At this point, the quartet did not even have a manager. A month passed after the Guarneri signed a recording contract with RCA before they signed up with Judson, O'Neill, Beall & Steinway to manage them. The firm is now known as Harry Beall Management, and Beall continues to represent them.

It was at their debut in the New School that Tree met his

wife, Jani. "At the time, I was enjoying my bachelorhood, and then I saw her in the audience," Tree has said. "As I recall, I blew a few notes. It turned out that she was with friends of mine, who brought her backstage after the concert. I knew within sixty seconds that I wanted to marry her, though it was a while before I actually did." Jani Tree, born in Austria, is an exceptionally pretty woman—as are all the Guarneri wives. She was only eighteen when they met. Tree says, "The life I lead wouldn't work for me at all if it weren't for Jani. She's my rock, my stability, my center of gravity."

Tree says that keeping their playing fresh is one of their main problems. "Sometimes we're tired and irritable, upset at having to be away so much, and we have to talk ourselves into the proper frame of mind—though we have life easier than musicians a quarter of a century ago. In the beginning, we were sometimes away for as much as two months. Now we wouldn't dream of being away for more than three weeks at a time. In the old days, three months was considered nothing. Of course, we miss out on those ship crossings you read about, when people like Kreisler and Schnabel had reunions, relaxed and enjoyed each other's company and the company of people in allied arts. We are able to get home the same day we've played a concert thousands of miles away. Still, it's the most beautiful way to spend one's life that I can imagine. It gets more and more exciting—*never* less. In a way, it's preaching—to play for an audience of two thousand people and to *touch* them, which is a very mysterious process. I think we are probably among the lucky one-tenth of one percent in the world who truly love and thrive on what they do for a living."

Tree recalls the quartet's tenth anniversary as one of the happiest days of his life. "It took a great deal of skill on the part of our friend Bill Lockwood, who is director of programming for Lincoln Center, to keep a cake out of our sight. We were all hovering around backstage. Philippe Entremont, the pianist, did a quintet with us, and he had to keep us collected at the door leading onstage and distract us. Onstage, Entremont took what I thought was an awfully long time getting himself adjusted at the piano, fixing his music, raising and lowering the piano bench. I wondered if he would ever stop fidgeting, when suddenly the stage door opened and Bill Lockwood came out pushing this enormous cake. We really were surprised. And the entire audience joined in singing 'Happy Birthday.' It was touching, and gratifying." Tree paused. "Well, we've had a lot of good moments. Nevertheless, it's a precarious existence. We are so dependent on each other."

~

John Dalley lays to rest for all time the pejorative connotation of the term "playing second fiddle." Quartets are often said to be as strong as the second violinist. Some music-lovers wish Dalley would quit the Guarneri and start his own quartet, and others fear he might. Dalley is the quiet one in the quartet. He never goes to post-concert parties—except in the Midwest, where he has friends, and where his heart is and always will be, according to Nancy Dalley—and the quartet members have such respect for each other's privacy that none of the others has ever asked him why. He's allergic to smoke, and that might be the reason. Also, he's very much a family man (he met Nancy at Curtis, where she was studying flute), and he is fiercely protective of what he considers his free time. Several years ago, the quartet was in London and so was Daniel Barenboim, the pianist and conductor, who was then the director of the South Bank Summer Music Festival, in London. Barenboim wanted the quartet to play at the festival the following summer—possibly a piano work with him. Harry Beall hoped the five would get together to discuss dates and programs, but they didn't. All four members of the Guarneri have friends in London and had scattered in four directions, so Beall set up a lunch date at the Plaza, in New York, on a Saturday when all five could be in the city. Dalley didn't show up. He sent word that it was his day off. After a New York concert, he's the first one out of the building, garment bag flying. Though they now wear dark suits and ties instead of white tie and tails—a shame, according to Beall, who says, "Coming onstage in white tie and tails, they looked like four wonderful devils"—they seem to feel imprisoned in formal clothing of any sort, and with the exception of Soyer, who won't carry a garment bag and a cello, they all change after a concert.

Dalley is sometimes more critical of how things are going during a rehearsal than the others. But when it is least expected, he can become a cutup, and it was he who initiated what they now call the "Bermuda riot." They all have slightly different versions of what happened, but Steinhardt's seems an accurate amalgamation. The quartet took their families to Bermuda. Bill Steckler, a lawyer, amateur violinist, and good friend, and Georgia Ruel, the Soyers's next-door neighbor in Babylon and Soyer's travel agent came, too. They anticipated a lovely time. They would be there for a week and had only four concerts to play. However, it rained steadily, and they found Bermudians stiff and unfriendly. And Tree, who is the unpaid personal manager and nagging conscience for them all, told Steckler during a walk on the beach, "They have the same schedule I have. I'm not going to make *any* phone calls this time. They can get where they should be under their own steam."

But Tree's phone rang so many times—calls from the others asking questions about rehearsals and programs—that he relented and went back to his usual role. They were asked to appear on a television talk show—something they don't often do—and they said they would. The weather was so lousy, they reasoned, they might as well—there wasn't anything else to do. Steinhardt has a musician friend who gets laughs at parties when he imitates talk-show hosts, and Steinhardt said the host—hostess, really—something of a local celebrity, was the essence of his comic friend: "Do you enjoy your work?" "What instruments do you play?" "Which one is the hardest?" "Do you get along with each other?" The program was underway and already sinking when Dalley spotted himself on the monitor and said, "Hey, look, guys! It's me!" He waved at the camera and said, "Hi, Mom!" The camera switched to Soyer, who was swiveling in his chair and admiring the squeak. Swift pan to Tree, who was blushing and trying to submerge himself in an appointment book the size of two postage stamps. He said, when asked what he was doing, "I forgot an appointment with Gentle Julius"—his dentist. Soyer said, "I want to sing 'Moon over Miami.'" Steinhardt says he thinks he was the only one who was behaving, though he couldn't help laughing, and when the hostess asked clumsily, "Are your wives happy?" Steinhardt drew himself up and in his best Erich von Stroheim hiss, said, "That, madam, is none of your business." Back to Dalley, who had taken to answering every question—"Do you travel together?" "Do you like Bermuda?"—with a stentorian "Never!" Pan to Soyer, who said, "This is getting *very* boring." Steinhardt says, "It was not nice of us; sometimes we get carried away, and one thing leads to another. In Tampa once, I hid behind a curtain and peeked out, and Dave said, 'Let's see your legs.' It was tasteless, zany, a little scandalous. I felt uncomfortable afterward. I thought we'd overstepped the bounds. We went to a restaurant later, and when we walked in, the room was suddenly bathed in silence. I'm sure we'll never be asked back."

Dalley, speaking of his own introduction to music, says, "I started violin lessons when I was four, with a man named Virgil Person. My family lived in Emporia, Kansas, at the time. My father, Orien, is a conductor, and he taught at Interlochen, the big music camp in Michigan. He also had a youth orchestra when we lived in Wichita. He believes in starting people young. I went to Interlochen summers, and I played a lot of quartets earlier than most. I began when I was fourteen, with three members of my father's youth symphony. He was kind enough to coach us once a week. Many musicians don't play chamber music until after college, which is a pity, because you can learn a lot about music and your instrument in chamber music. I did my best work between fifteen and eighteen, before Curtis.

"I had met the Czech violinist Ottokar Čadek at Interlochen one summer. He taught at the University of Alabama, and he invited me to come and live with him and his family. My parents, who were then living in Ann Arbor, let me go, and it was the best thing they ever did for me. Mr. Čadek had an in-residence quartet at school, and I got familiar with most of the quartet literature just listening to them rehearse and give concerts. I went to school half days, and practiced the rest of the time. Mrs. Čadek was an excellent violinist, so even my practice was supervised, since she was always at home. I knew someone was listening, so I couldn't fool around, and I learned to do things right. My teacher warned me about Curtis—the big talents I would encounter—so I wasn't quite as shocked as some of the other new students.

Mike and I both studied with Efrem Zimbalist, and Arnold studied with Ivan Galamian. I played first and second in quartets at Curtis. We were interchanging all the time, which gives you a good sense of what the other voices do. The second-violin syndrome so many people talk about—a feeling of inferiority . . . It's hard to say whether playing second makes people that way or if they were that way to begin with. I think Sasha would have quit the Budapest even if he'd played first. It's his personality. He wanted to do other things. I enjoy playing violin in piano quartets—it's like reading something just for pleasure. If I hadn't played first earlier in my life a great deal, I might have a different temperamental outlook. But I've done solo playing and first, and I don't have a burning desire to do either." Dalley had a concert career similar to Tree's, playing concertos with symphony orchestras and touring in other countries, including the Soviet Union.

"I think everyone in the quartet is indispensable," Dalley says. "It's true that I do most of the leading when Arnold doesn't. Anything involving the lower three voices is my responsibility—except in instances when the second violin is out of the picture completely—both melodically and rhythmically. The Budapest worked that way. Their first violinist, Joseph Roisman, didn't like to lead—he wasn't comfortable doing it —so Sasha took up the slack. They were probably the first democratic quartet."

Dalley has a reputation for doing everything just the right way, in terms of not only musicianship but muscle use. He says, "I don't know about that. I play golf and I don't do it right, but then I think a golf swing is the most intricate thing I can think of—next to holding a bow. You may think you have a natural swing if it feels right, but there are a thousand and one things you can do wrong. It's diabolical. But I've learned to relax. I can play golf for pleasure, without smashing my driver into the ground.

"We get tired of a work we've toured with, but we play such good music we don't get *sick* of it. The other day, we were all complaining about the Schubert, but it was a question of physical fatigue—not the kind of fatigue that sets in with boredom. Some of the Mozart quartets sound as if he set out to write an exercise; others are exhilarating. Haydn is always fresh, and a Beethoven seems brand-new every time we play it."

Dalley doesn't seem to get the pleasure out of travel that the others do, and he says, "I don't *enjoy* it, but if you're going to play concerts you have to travel. If I ever quit, it wouldn't be because of travel but because I want to do something else. But we hope to gradually cut down on the number of concerts we do. As you get older, you lose some of your strength. We used to do as many as a hundred and thirty. It got abnormally out of hand."

Nancy and John Dalley toured some Iron Curtain countries—East Germany, Yugoslavia—with the Robert Shaw Chorale, and John was in Russia for the 1962 Tchaikovsky Competition. He says the quartet has been invited many times to tour Russia, but the conditions were never acceptable to them: they would be expected to stay longer than they want to, and they would be paid in rubles, which they could not take out of the country.

Before the quartet was formed, Dalley and his wife taught at Oberlin and they were artists-in-residence at the University of Illinois. Dalley also taught at Curtis, and currently, along with the others, does some coaching on tour. Tree, who has witnessed Dalley in action, says he is the consummate teacher, with a rare ability to get to a problem immediately. Dalley quit Curtis to have more time to spend with his family. "With three children—each with special needs—it's not right to be away so much," he says. "I spend as much time with them as I possibly can."

Of the four, he is the only one who has encouraged his children to be musicians. Karen, now nineteen, was given piano lessons, but Dalley felt he and Nancy didn't push her enough. She still plays, but her main interest is art. Kirsten, twelve, is studying cello and they intend to push her for a few years. Her teacher is Kathryn Brainard, a ferocious perfectionist, but Kirsten likes her and is not impatient. Dalley sits in on the lessons, as Mrs. Brainard requires of her pupils' parents. Soon the Dalleys will know whether she is a big talent or just a good cellist: she is developing a vibrato, and her musicianship—her musical expression—will begin to reveal itself. Dalley is not alone in feeling that vibrato is the key to the sound a string player produces. Of the age-old debate over which is more difficult, the left hand or the right, bow arm, he says, "I could certainly play the left-hand part of the Paganini Caprice No. 5, but without a lot of practicing I'm not sure I could bow it." In a year or so, Erik will begin music lessons, most probably violin.

Dalley is learning to practice without using the violin—an idea he got from his friend the pianist Lee Luvisi. Luvisi told Dalley he could work out fingerings, phrasings, in his head, without wearing himself out at the keyboard, and even memorize scores by looking at the music. Dalley doesn't need to memorize the literature, but he has found the approach valuable in other respects.

For his own pleasure, Dalley makes violin bows in his spare time, and takes the necessary equipment on the road to work on a bow in his hotel room after a concert. The right wood—aged twenty-five years—is hard to come by. Bowmakers who own it don't want to part with it. Dalley has made sixty bows. He sells a few to friends, and for the most part he uses his own bows.

~

David Soyer—a cousin of the renowned painters Moses, Raphael, and Isaac Soyer—didn't start cello lessons until he was eleven, rather late for a virtuoso performer. "My older sister played piano, but neither of my parents was a musician," he says, "and there wasn't anyone in particular shoving me in that direction. There weren't many competitions in those days. The Philadelphia Orchestra had one—still does—that I won. The prize was getting to play a concerto with the orchestra. I gave six or eight recitals in New York. Musically, there isn't anything I haven't done. I was in the first 'Ed Sullivan Show' orchestra, I was a member of the CBS Symphony, and I did jingles and commercials. I met my wife, Janet, who plays harp, on one of those jobs twenty-one years ago. I recorded with a Pachanga band, and even played for a chimpanzee act. I believe every musical experience is enriching and contributes to a total development. After all, both Casals and Kreisler played in cafés. There are waltzes in Haydn and Mozart. How can you do them really well if you've never played a waltz?

"My first professional quartet experience was with the Guilet Quartet. Then I joined the New Music Quartet. But there wasn't the demand for quartets then that there is now. The New Music and the Juilliard were the only important American quartets then, and, of course, the Budapest was playing mostly in America. The New Music gave sixty-five or seventy concerts a year, many of them in schools for young audiences—a program designed to get youngsters interested in music, familiar with it. But at our peak I think we each ended up with six thousand dollars a year, because the fees were so low. The Budapest, the greatest quartet in the world

at the time, charged eight hundred. I think they were afraid
to ask for more, for fear the number of concerts would dwin-
dle."

The three others in the Guarneri have said that Soyer is
so casual about money that they could rob him blind if they
chose to. When informed of the remark, Soyer looked surprised, thought for a moment, and then laughed. "It's true,"
he said. "When Janet and I were playing commercials, our
income was about thirty-five thousand a year. When I turned
to chamber music, our income dropped to nothing and gradually climbed. Neither one of us was bothered by the change."

Soyer and Tree were in the Marlboro Trio for four years
before the quartet was formed. "There is nowhere near the
demand for piano trios that there is for quartets," Soyer has
said. "The piano-trio literature, though good, is more limited,
and somehow there doesn't seem to be public acceptance of
the idea of a trio as an ensemble. Not like quartets, which have
to be so cohesive. Trio writing is more soloistic, and the
ensemble problems are not as difficult or sensitive as they are
in quartets. The truth is, a piano doesn't really blend with
strings. On a piano, F-sharp and G-flat are the same note. With
a string instrument, the sharp could be a bit sharper and the
flat a bit flatter, depending on the key you're playing in. Casals
called it 'expressive intonation.' When we play a piano quartet
or quintet, we make an adjustment of sorts; it's almost sub-
conscious. But then there's always an adjustment of intonation
between one string player and another. Every player has a
somewhat different intonation."

When they rehearsed with Peter Serkin for concerts in
Vancouver, Soyer played a phrase for Serkin that they would
do together, to demonstrate an inflection he thought the
phrase needed. Serkin said wistfully, "I envy your intonation." There are marvelous works for piano and strings that

they enjoy doing, and they have played with thirty-five or forty of the best pianists, though Tree says, "Sometimes the pianist gets nervous and lets go and we have to fight to be heard. It's like being doused with gallons of maple syrup."

Soyer says, "We like playing a variety of things, doing works that call for other instruments." Of an occasion when they linked up with the Vermeer, in residence at the University of Northern Illinois, to play the Mendelssohn Octet, Soyer said, "There was, of course, a clash of styles. Theirs is much more delicate. We're bigger, stronger, and louder, and we more or less shouted them down." He laughed when he talked about it, and added, "We amaze them—our outspokenness. They think we're a bunch of gangsters. We kid them a lot—we call them the Veh-is-Mir or the Veneer Quartet. Actually, they did defer to us, probably because as a quartet we're older and more experienced. But they are *so* polite to one another."

Soyer has a favorite story that illustrates the difficulty of giving and accepting criticism, the importance of not taking it personally. It concerns the Amadeus Quartet and the violist Cecil Aronowitz, who played quintets with them. They had just finished an exhausting tour, and when it was over they began a long stretch of recording sessions. "They were all tired," as Soyer tells it, "and during the final session Martin Lovett, the cellist, said to Aronowitz, 'Cecil, you played that like a pig.' Aronowitz was terribly offended, and he said, 'All right, that's it. I will never play with you guys again.' Nobody paid much attention to the scene, and they finished the recording session. Months later, they were about to go on another tour—quintets again—and the Amadeus violist, Peter Schidlof, called Aronowitz to give him the schedule. Aronowitz said, 'But I told you I was never going to play with you again.' Schidlof said, 'Why not?' and Aronowitz said, 'Martin said I played like a pig,' and Schidlof said, 'Yes, but why aren't you going to play with us?' " The story gets shaggier and shaggier as each member gets the same response from Aronowitz that Schidlof did. Soyer said, "The Amadeus is accustomed to talking like that, and no one takes it personally. Cecil had been accepted by them, and they were completely bewildered by his attitude."

Of works the Guarneri plays, Soyer says, "There are pieces we have performed that some of us have grown to hate. Some pieces one member didn't like from the start, and we'd never do those again. That big Schubert, the G Major, almost put us away. It's so long—forty-five minutes of steady playing, with possibly a total of eight bars' rest in the entire piece. Then, too, it is very difficult playing at such an intense level. It's emotionally taxing. The sheer physical exertion required, the muscle control. There are tremolos, fortes, stormy passages, loud, explosive things. Of course, it's a fantastic work, a great piece. One of Schubert's most important works. I strained my right arm, and a slight numbness in my right side stayed with me for months."

Beall gives the Guarneri its schedule late in the summer, and in recent years they have asked him to limit engagements, to turn some invitations down. "We said, 'Stop! No more!' " Soyer says. "The 1976–77 season was horrendous: from September to July—one hundred and twenty-five concerts, plus eight days' recording, plus teaching, plus daily rehearsals. A very tiring season." Even so, Soyer played at Bowdoin College, in Maine, for two weeks during his vacation that summer. He taught master classes for five of the more advanced students, and he gave a recital.

Of the four, Soyer is the only one who is able to take his wife along when she wants to go. They have no children. He has two grown sons by a first marriage. Janet Soyer is a tall, slim, exceptionally attractive woman, with a broad streak of generosity in her—sensitivity too. All of the quartet's New York concerts are sold out well in advance, but each member gets two tickets. On rare occasions—usually at the last minute —Mrs. Soyer finds herself with an extra ticket. She goes to the concert and waits near the box office and scrutinizes the people milling around in hopes of getting a ticket that someone has turned in. She almost always finds an eager student who will be grateful for the chance to hear the concert and surprised that it's free. Occasionally, the student, not knowing who she is, will compare the Guarneri unfavorably with the Amadeus or an upcoming group. Mrs. Soyer is an artist as well as a musician, and Harry Beall has in his office, on loan, a portrait she did of her husband. Beall likes the painting so much that he does not intend to return it—at least not voluntarily.

Soyer studied with Diran Alexanian, a colleague of Casals, and with Emanuel Feuermann. He later had coaching sessions with Casals. Some years ago, the Russian cellist Mstislav Rostropovich started using a curved, longer peg that raised the instrument three or four inches. He felt it not only made thumb positions easier but tilted the cello slightly, and thus projected the sound outward to the audience. It swept the cello world, and a large number of cellists now use it. Soyer tried it and didn't like it. He says, "Any benefit gained by making thumb positions easier is lost; first position is harder, the hand gets numb. Also, it looks sloppy."

Like Tree, Soyer considers quartet playing more difficult than a solo performance. "There's no question about it—it's tenser, more nerve-racking," he says. "It's true that if one makes a mistake the others are sympathetic. A wrong note, a wrong entrance, a slip of the finger, a lapse in concentration —a problem for all of us, especially when we're very tired. But concentration can become habitual, part of the technique of performing. And concentration in itself does away with nervousness. Nervousness is a funny thing. I think performers who suffer most fear the *idea* of nervousness. Experienced performers accept the fact that it is part of what they do. If you're going to run around the block, you're going to pant; if you're going to perform, you're going to be nervous. It's not the most comfortable feeling in the world, but it can actually work for you. If there is no nervousness, chances are the performance will be bland. Nerves create excitement, spontaneity, which is translated to the audience as vitality."

Rumors persist that the quartet is about to split up. Soyer is amused that the rumors sometimes result from the fact that when they're at a party they talk to other people instead of to each other. He says, "I think we've weathered all the storms that could possibly come up by now. It's really those first five years—like pebbles being polished in a grinding machine, knocking against each other—that are the most difficult ones. Now we know each other's foibles and frailties. We all know we're lucky to play quartets for a living—and a damned good living, too." Their friend William Steckler, who is the founder and director of the Roslyn, Long Island, chamber-music series and is in a position to know, says they are the highest-paid quartet in the world. They make no claim to altruism, but in the course of raising their fee they have helped other quartets to do the same. "It's hard work, though the fact that we're successful helps," according to Soyer. "If we were struggling and clawing away, it would be doubly difficult. We've never had to worry about having enough engagements, though it took quite a while to get the fee up to something we could live on. And we have devoted followers all over the world, and some have become good friends. It makes all the travel more palatable."

Soyer says the quartet takes political stands when they all

are in agreement. "We played at anti-Vietnam War rallies, and we like to help out political candidates—fund-raising, mostly," he says. "So far, they've all been losers—McGovern, Allard Lowenstein, Paul O'Dwyer, a few others. I think we're known as the kiss of death." They were offered an exceptionally lucrative tour in South Africa, and they told Beall to refuse, to say that they didn't want to play there because of apartheid. Back came a letter saying, "We would be happy to arrange for you to play for blacks, too." They read mail meant for all of them at rehearsals. That letter was wadded up and pitched into a wastebasket.

Soyer considers teaching a responsibility, and he averages about ten pupils a year. "It's a lot for me, but somehow I manage to fit them all in. I've been teaching really seriously for the past ten years. Before that, I always taught a few, in a rather sporadic fashion. I enjoy it very much, and find it challenging, and also very difficult. I don't have a 'method.' Sometimes I wish I did. I don't have a *set* method in the sense that all the students do Popper No. 3, Piatti No. 2, this étude, that exercise. Some teachers do that—a very structured approach. I feel I do better trying to meet a particular student's individual needs, taking into account what strengths and weaknesses he has. I try to correct the weaknesses and enforce the strengths, even if they are not the kind of strengths I would have preferred. I think I'm rather tolerant about that. It's a bit more demanding, paying such attention to the individual. It takes more thought, and it's also more frustrating. I think a sincere teacher feels that if a student isn't doing well, it's his fault. He feels he isn't explaining things well. He's failing a student in some fashion, which is frustrating. When it works, when things are going well, teaching is extremely satisfying."

He spoke of one student: "He's very talented, but he

doesn't trust his instincts, which is a problem. Many talented musicians depend more on their instincts than on their intellect. He's the other way around, though he has perfectly good instincts. He's suspicious of using them. The ideal situation would be a good balance of the two—instinctual and intellectual musicality, with some tempering of one by the other. It can't be all one or the other."

Soyer will refuse a pupil he doesn't find interesting or one he feels is hopeless. "I've accepted pupils and then discovered they're hopeless. I try to dismiss them as diplomatically as possible: 'You might be happier with another teacher.' 'Maybe you should think about getting a degree.' He laughed. 'Perhaps a doctorate—in archeology.'

"I feel very strongly that since I've studied with some of the greatest, I should pass on what I've been taught—pass along the message, so to speak. We're losing our traditions rapidly in society as well as in music. Students these days lack an exposure to European, Middle European traditions—gypsy music, folk music. So much of the literature—Haydn, Mozart, Schubert, Beethoven—is based on those things. German, Hungarian, Viennese tunes. Students have no knowledge or experience of that music. Most of them have never heard gypsy violinists in their lives. There's a strong current of that in string playing. All those composers heard such music and were affected by it. There are trios in Haydn quartets, movements to be played *à la zingaresca,* rondos, Austrian waltz-like tunes. Music that comes from the mountains and the countryside. These kids have never heard music like that. They've obviously heard Haydn, Mozart, Beethoven, but they haven't heard the *antecedents* of those composers' music. And there's no *way* for them to hear it, unless they go to Europe. And even in Europe it isn't often heard. I feel young musicians are growing up in a musically antiseptic atmosphere. I had a rich past given to me, because I associated with musicians of great stature who came from that kind of background. I feel I should pass it along, to the extent that I can. There's an ego thing, too, in teaching. You want to transmit your *own* ideas. You want your ideas propagated."

One of Soyer's students won a competition whose award was a number of concerts—possibly an instant career. Soyer felt he wasn't quite ready, and continued to teach the young man free of charge. He still comes to Soyer for advice and, according to Soyer, is doing very well. "He's a good kid," Soyer says. "Very gifted."

Soyer was in the Navy "exactly three years and seven months," during the Second World War, and spent that time in the United States Navy Band—which was founded by an act of Congress, he likes to point out, and for which he learned to play a baritone horn, the euphonium. He also played cello in the band's sister orchestra, which gave concerts every Friday night, and had for its concertmaster the renowned musician's musician Oscar Shumsky (Soyer says Shumsky taught him everything he knows about bowing) and for its first oboe the Metropolitan Opera orchestra's first oboist, William Arrowsmith.

Soyer talks about this experience: "Lateness was frowned upon, but Arrowsmith was an oversleeper. He just couldn't get up in the morning, and he was late three mornings in a row. The commanding officer said, 'That's it!' And Arrowsmith was court-martialed—he was sentenced to a week in the brig. We needed him for rehearsals and concerts, so two big Marines would march him, under guard, to the hall. Guns were trained on him while he was playing, and then he'd be marched back to the brig. Shuffling along, carrying his oboe case, flanked by those two huge Marines carrying Garand rifles, he looked funny to us. *He* didn't think it was funny.

When the week was up, the Navy moved him in with a wind player who *could* get up in the morning—get himself up, and Arrowsmith too."

Mornings, the band played music for officers' calisthenics, and during the winter, on bitter-cold days, Soyer says the band members all ate hot, hot chili at seven in the morning to warm themselves, their mouths especially, for outdoor playing. "We were standing still; those guys were jumping around."

Soyer and Dalley were in the first American Quartet, under the aegis of Sol Hurok Management. But Hurok, who liked big productions—ballet companies, circuses, and the like—lost interest in the quartet almost before the ink was dry on their contract. The demise of the quartet, marked by an exchange of letters canceling what few concerts they did have, is commemorated by a framed print of the famous "This marks the end of the Schwarzwälder String Quartet" cartoon, with the letters affixed to the back, hanging in the Soyers' apartment in Manhattan.

Soyer's second love is sailing—he claims half the things he reads have to do with sailing, though he's exaggerating; he's a fountain of facts gleaned from all the airplane reading he's done over the years. However, someone visiting the Soyers at their summer home on Long Island is apt—if he or she has arrived too late to go for a sail—to end up sitting in Soyer's twenty-four-foot sloop, moored in a canal a few yards from the house, talking there rather than in the Soyers' living room.

~

Many people feel that Arnold Steinhardt's beauty of phrasing and sweetness of tone are special with him, a major contribution to the quartet's overall character and sound. After their debut, an amateur violinist said to a friend, "If Mephistopheles appeared and asked what I wanted in exchange for my soul, I would say, 'To sound like Arnold Steinhardt.' "

Steinhardt grew up in Los Angeles, and he speaks with what he describes as a typical California non-accent. His parents emigrated from Poland, and his father, Steinhardt says, did "a million things in his life." He was an engraver, a diamond-setter. He bought and sold old gold door to door. He eventually owned a liquor store—the last thing he did before he retired. "My parents got me started," Steinhardt says. "They're not musicians, but they are music-lovers. I think they thought it would be a very nice thing for us to be musicians—my brother, Victor, and I. He's six years younger and a pianist. Music is one of the values my mother would capitalize, like Justice, Truth, Beauty.

"Both of my parents had this idea about excellence, about doing something with yourself. If it wasn't music it would have been something else—a lofty endeavor, what they thought of as a 'service field,' where we could do something for other people—a doctor, a lawyer, an educator, a scientist. If we hadn't been gifted in music, they would have been happy to say, 'Give it up.' Some kids don't need a push. Jaime Laredo's parents didn't push him. He practiced on his own. He has a tremendous gift. But I would often get in hot water. My parents would catch me practicing with a book on my stand—reading and faking the practice. They gave me a push —an important push.

"I started lessons when I was six. My parents rented a violin for me for a dollar, which they got back at the end of the year—the result of an effort in the school I was going to to start an orchestra. After the first year, I was taught by Carl Moldren, who specialized in teaching children. Many of his pupils went on to professional careers. I had an immediate response to music—loved it from the start—and I felt a kind of romance with the public from the beginning. I thought it

54

was exciting, as a kid of seven, playing with other students. I was nervous at first, but I felt a rush of pleasure as things began to go well onstage, and afterward, when all the relatives told me how nicely I had played, I was quite pleased.

"After Mr. Moldren, I had a couple of Leopold Auer teachers. One of them, Peter Meremblum, had a youth orchestra in Los Angeles that I played in. He had come to Los Angeles to play in studio orchestras, and he knew everybody in the music world. He was temperamental, had a thick Russian accent. The kids were frightened of him and loved him at the same time. There are literally hundreds of first-desk orchestra musicians who were in his youth orchestra at one time. He was chummy with Heifetz, Piatigorsky, Rubinstein. When they were in town, they would come and play with our orchestra. I remember the day Rubinstein came to play with us. He stopped in the middle of a concerto and said, 'You'll have to forgive me'—typical Rubinstein—'I know I'm playing terribly. I was up much too late last night, and I had much too much to drink.' This to thirteen- and fourteen-year-olds. He passed himself off as a charming scoundrel. He said, 'I don't need this rehearsal. I need two aspirin.' Everybody loved him.

"When I was fifteen, I studied with Toscha Seidel, a pupil of Leopold Auer. He was the concertmaster of the Paramount Studios orchestra, and I stayed with him until I went to Curtis. Most of us arrived at Curtis with delusions of grandeur—but we soon learned that we had been big fish in a little pond. The wonderful thing about Curtis is that it cuts you down to size right away. Everyone is very good, and everyone is working *hard,* and that's as much a factor in your education as who your teacher is. I studied with Ivan Galamian, and I stayed for five years. During the last two, I did some playing, and entered some competitions. I never dreamed I'd be a string-quartet player. I didn't have any formed ideas.

55

"I still get nervous when I play, and I'm pleased when it goes well, though I don't get as nervous playing quartets. There's a responsibility in quartets, but you're not so nakedly delivered up as you are when you play solo. In many senses, though, quartets are more difficult—one slip and you can throw the others off. In a recital with a pianist, the piano sound can cover a multitude of sins. It's as if you were let out of school for fun and games. There's much more latitude. Quartets demand such discipline. There are passages in the inner voices that have to be absolutely right and are extremely difficult to execute—harder than getting up and playing a solo. It's all in the mind, what's difficult, and when I get nervous it's for psychological, not technical, reasons. I think you go through cycles in your life—in and out of periods when you're more or less secure with your playing. It has to do with other things in your life. I was insecure when I was a student at Curtis, but gradually I developed a certain amount of confidence. When we play our standard repertoire, pieces scheduled for a season, it's a wonderful feeling to sit down with these old friends— Beethoven, Mozart. We've practiced all the difficult parts and we sit down and make music together. Possibly there are spots —the perfect ritard, the precise diminuendo—that we should pay more attention to, but I think you give up more than you get by practicing for total perfection. We do try to be true to a musical ideal that we look for in each piece.

"Music in itself is a reward, and when our families come along—Bermuda, Florida, a resort in Switzerland—it can be a magical thing. We go to some pretty god-awful places in the world, but then the pendulum swings and we're dining with the Duke of Someplace—one extreme to the other. In the beginning, I got tired of it. It was in my bachelor days, and I wasn't used to touring. There is such a sense of alienation, traveling so much. Days lose their usual distinction. Sundays are like Tuesdays, Saturdays like Mondays. Sometimes I had myself paged in airports to give myself the feeling that there was someone there who knew me. Once, we were in one of those drab, faceless cities and I was profoundly depressed. I complained to Dave, and he wasn't sympathetic. He got mad. He said, 'You don't dare complain! You don't know how lucky you are to be a musician doing what you're doing.'

"He was right, of course. I find life easier now that I have a family to come home to. I feel I could go on a five-year voyage and when I returned they would be waiting for me." Steinhardt married Dorothea van Haeften in 1970. A professional photographer, born in Germany, she spoke very little English when they met, at her sister's home, in Buffalo, and Steinhardt spoke very little German. Each studied the other's language, and they met somewhere in the middle. They have two children—a daughter, Natasha, who is nine, and a three-year-old son, Alexander.

The conductor George Szell was one of the judges of the Leventritt International Competition the year Steinhardt won. The competition is often a springboard to a solo career, but Steinhardt felt that he wasn't ready—that he was still too green. Szell lured him into the Cleveland Orchestra with promises—fulfilled—of solo performances with the orchestra and lessons with Joseph Szigeti, in Switzerland. "I expected to go over there and talk about the architecture of music—high-minded discussions," Steinhardt has said. "But Szigeti wanted to talk about the fiddle—like everybody else in my life. I thought: Enough about the fiddle. Let's talk about music. It took a bit of an adjustment, but ultimately we talked a great deal about music, though he went about it obliquely rather than in grand terms. We worked on repertoire, and it all unfolded wonderfully. I still remember vividly many things he said about different pieces. It was toward the end of his life, and he was a sick man. It must have been difficult for him. He'd retired from the concert stage, and yet the violin was everything to him.

"Playing in the Cleveland was a great thrill at first—the repertoire, sitting next to Josef Gingold, the concertmaster. But I began to feel I was a cog in a machine, and Szell got to me. He was so compulsively orderly in his musical interpretations. I felt it took precedence over the great colors, fluidity, flexibility in the music. Once in a while we had a great performance. The orchestra was fantastic, and that was all Szell's doing. He was a fine administrator, a pedagogue. But in retrospect, I don't think he was really a great musician.

"Marlboro was the most marvelous musical experience of my life. Everything I learned there is reflected in any music I play. I met so many different people, got involved in such a variety of musical situations. When we decided to be a quartet, I didn't know Dave well, though I'd played a couple of piano trios with him. We were absolutely sure of ourselves as a quartet. There was no sense of doubt about any member. It was extraordinary. If anyone should quit, I can't imagine finding a replacement—except for me. I would be the easiest to replace. Everybody has a very strong sense of himself—his musical self—in our group, which is why it's possible for us to play without a leader.

"I mark bowings in parts, because we want to do the same things, but I've got a bugaboo about fingerings. I rarely use the same ones. I enjoy the play, the creativity. It's not a question of fooling around. If you have a slightly different musical idea, you may want to implement it with another fingering. Of course, there are some passages that can only be fingered one way, but for the bulk of the repertoire you have many different choices at any given moment."

Steinhardt looks extremely relaxed when he plays, but he

says, "There was a time in my life when I was in a great deal of pain. It's difficult for me to play the violin. I work hard at it. It's like a sport—tennis, for example. The most efficient, economic, natural, the least encumbered way is the way to do it. Halfway through the quartet's life, I got in terrible trouble. Neck pains, back pains, finger pains, muscle spasms. Partly because I'd broken my right wrist playing tennis, and it was difficult for me to make an adjustment afterward. You're never quite the same after you've broken a bone, and I had to learn to play much more efficiently." He also learned to play tennis left-handed, to spare his vulnerable right arm. "Early in life you can do things improperly and get away with it, but as you get older your joints are not as flexible. I went to a number of doctors, checked into a hospital for ten days for tests, saw a psychiatrist. I even tried mud baths in Germany."

The late Imre Waldbauer, whose Hungarian Quartet was one of the best in Europe until the Second World War brought it to a halt—Bartók dedicated his second quartet to them—took a year's sabbatical and studied anatomy in Paris with Rodin in search of a solution to the constant pain that accompanied his career. He learned *why* he hurt so much but not how to avoid it entirely. Steinhardt says "I worked for hours with my friend Shmuel Ashkenasi, the first violinist of the Vermeer, whose musicianship and technique I greatly respect. He would sit in the first row in the audience during concerts and study my bow arm. Afterward, he'd say, 'It *looks* right,' but then he'd suggest a different way to hold the bow, apply pressure, and it was fruitful. But it was a terrible time. I thought my career was over. Other musicians avoid you; they're afraid the same thing might happen to them, and they don't want to talk about it. I was in pain all the time. It's much better now. I no longer have spasms and inflammations, and I think it is from learning to play more efficiently. It's also partly a mental attitude. It's hard enough to play the violin well, and if you're tense it's even harder. I don't want to sound like a Zen disciple, but it's better to just let it happen, let everything function as smoothly as possible. Just look at John. He's a study in ease, the way his limbs work, his fingers. Anything he does is so natural, and it's partly the way he's put together. I have to work for it. I don't want to sound immodest—I'm gifted. But I've always had to work very hard."

Dalley thinks many of Steinhardt's problems are a result of the fact that he's so tall. "Holding a violin is unnatural, against gravity," Dalley says. "Everyone must adjust to it— scrunch the shoulder up, press down with the chin. For Arnold it's especially unnatural." Steinhardt says, "I also think part of the trouble is that in quartets there are more technical demands for me than there are in being a soloist. Certain bow strokes, tiny little figures with a small amount of bow. You never have to do things that delicate in a concerto, when you're painting on a big broad canvas, with long strokes. In chamber music, lush, Romantic music is easier, because there's the big gesture. The exacting fine points in Mozart and Schubert are more difficult, though that Schubert was easier for me than it was for the others, who had those accompanying figures that go on and on, those tremolos. I'm exhausted after playing it—there's so much to do—but it's more an emotional exhaustion.

"We get along better now than we did at first. All kinds of things have been worked through. You're criticized constantly when you're in a quartet. No one ever tells you you play beautifully. In one of our question periods after an open rehearsal, one of the students asked if we ever complimented one another. It set us back on our heels to realize that we never did. If John should say to me, 'That was beautiful,' I'd get very nervous and think something was really wrong. If Dave said, 'That was fine,' I'd wonder: What did he *really* mean? In general, we just expect that everyone should play really well. We've had many heated arguments in the group, and not quietly, either, though I don't think there are any lingering hard feelings. You learn how to give criticism in a good way, and to understand how each member operates best, what his style is. If Dave says, with that glowering look of his, 'That was rotten,' the first time you think: Why does he do that? Why can't he be more polite? But when you've known Dave fifteen years, you realize that more often than not that's just his way of being funny, and he doesn't mean anything personal. John has his way, and Michael his, and you begin to interpret the criticism by itself, without any ugly little creatures attached. Sometimes talk is very dangerous, because music is not a verbal language, and when you start to talk about it too much you get into dangerous waters. I think that's why most music criticism and most of the comment and description about it are difficult at best, and most often boring. I'd been playing quartets for ten years, and I read a book about the Beethoven quartets and I didn't know what in the world the author was talking about.''

Steinhardt likes to give solo recitals, and he does about four or five a season. He is constantly learning new repertoire, which is quite unusual, considering how busy the quartet is. He says that he has learned to make every minute count, and that he practices in odd places and at strange times to get in a few minutes here, a few minutes there. Once, he was practicing in a men's room in the Sydney, Australia, airport. Two guards rushed in and asked what he thought he was doing. Steinhardt said, "I'm practicing. Is it against the law?" One of the guards shrugged and said, "There is no precedent."

~

The Guarneri is known for, among other things, a warm, silken, seamless sound, which cannot be attributed to the instruments they play. Steinhardt has used five different violins over the past fourteen years. Soyer's Andrea Guarneri—the first Guarneri in the Guarneri—is now valued at one hundred and fifty thousand dollars and the value is escalating rapidly. The others play comparatively modest instruments for a group of their stature.

Steinhardt played a Guarneri for a year or so, but he didn't really like it, so he turned it over to the violin dealer Jacques Français, who sold it for Steinhardt for a handsome sum. (Purchasers request anonymity these days. They don't want to run the risk of being robbed.) Steinhardt is now playing an instrument made by Lorenzo Storioni, in Cremona, which belonged to Joseph Roisman. Steinhardt had always liked the sound when he listened to the Budapest, and after Roisman's death he bought the instrument. He says he likes it because it already knows all the repertoire. Steinhardt says the E string is the weakest—many instruments have one string weaker than the others—and some dealers who have examined it think it might be a cut-down viola. (Steinhardt has said that he thinks program notes should include the fact that he plays the only instrument in the world that has undergone a sex-change operation.) The E string bothers him, but he has grown accustomed to playing out on it—applying more energy to that string than to the others. Over the years, many violin scrolls have been broken or stolen, and the absence of the original scroll diminishes the value of an instrument by thirty percent. Steinhardt's violin was worth twenty thousand dollars. The scroll is another matter. Français suspects it may be the work of a Guarneri, and if he would put his opinion in writing, the scroll would be worth about thirty thousand dollars—if Steinhardt could find the owner of a Guarneri that does not have its original scroll. However, in 1979 Français found a Storioni scroll for Steinhardt, bringing the value of the instrument to twenty-eight thousand.

Dalley plays a Nicolas Lupot—called a French Strad, because Lupot copied the Stradivari. It cost Dalley thirty-five hundred dollars in 1963 and is probably worth over ten times that figure now. Tree's viola is a Dominicus Busan, worth sixty-five thousand. At one time, the quartet was offered the use of matched Strads, and then matched Amatis, but they liked their own instruments better. Also, they feel rather strongly that composers wrote for four voices and that the four should have distinctive sounds.

All have tried different bows along the way. One day, Tree was teaching his son the rudiments of baseball, using a rubber ball and his bow as a bat. He whacked the ball and broke the tip off the bow. Dalley went with him to help pick another. Tree bought the first one he tried—said he could tell immediately that it would suit him. Dalley was horrified. He said, "For God's sake, Mike, a man spends more time than that picking out a tie." Tree didn't tell Dalley that he is much more particular about his tennis equipment.

All four keep one hand or both eyes on their instruments at all times. The instruments are insured, of course, but with cash in hand, they would still be hard to replace. Walter Trampler's viola, which he left next to his luggage in a hotel lobby in San Francisco once during a tour, was missing when Trampler got to the airport. He went to the police, and the story made the afternoon edition of the *Chronicle,* front page. It probably wouldn't have occurred to the hotel barber who had found the instrument in the lobby to ask for ransom, but he saw the write-up and the figure $150,000, and he succumbed to a spasm of larceny. He sent a note to Trampler, who had canceled his flight and returned to the same hotel, asking for twenty thousand dollars. But he was an amateur larcenist, and agreed that two insurance agents could be present when the exchange was to be made in Trampler's hotel room. The agents stood by while the barber counted the money three times. Then they identified themselves as policemen, and arrested him.

Soyer came to a rehearsal one day with a new cello. He said he liked it, but the others were skeptical. (Steinhardt has tried a new instrument a couple of times, but the initial enthusiasm soon wears off when the excitement of the fresh sound gives way to an awareness of flaws.) Horacio Pinerio, an Argentinian who works in Français's shop, had taken the measurements of Soyer's Guarneri while it was in the shop for repairs, and copied it. The new instrument didn't have the major flaw that its Guarneri model has. The latter is so wide across the top that it's not possible to get a properly curved bridge, with the result that, to avoid playing on two strings at once, while playing on one string Soyer must press down on an adjoining string. This sounds nightmarish—like running a marathon with a sprained ankle—but Soyer is used to it, and it bothers him not at all. Soyer procrastinated about buying the new cello. He thought he'd rather have a new boat. Eventually he did buy it, though he doesn't always use it. He says, "It's really an excellent cello, with a big, open, free sound, a good quality. It carries in a hall, responds well, looks good. But I find I get tired of the sound. It's too *uncomplicated.* It's like those Rheingold girls—they were very pretty, but they were too perfect. They were insipid. They all looked alike."

PART III

Peter Marsh, the first violinist of the Lenox Quartet, which succeeded the Guarneri as quartet-in-residence at Harpur College, says the Guarneri is New York City's quartet-in-residence. In fact, the Guarneri does about twenty-five concerts in the city during the season, in five different auditoriums.

Hilde Limondjian, now program manager of the Metropolitan Museum's Grace Rainey Rogers Department of Concerts and Lectures, heard the Guarneri in their first appearance as a quartet, at Marlboro, in 1964. The program manager at the time was Dr. William Kolodney, and both Dr. Kolodney and Miss Limondjian knew Tree and Steinhardt as violinists; Tree had appeared on their Introduction Series in 1959 (a series sponsored by the Martha Baird Rockefeller Foundation to provide young artists with an opportunity to perform in public), and Steinhardt on the 1961 series. Miss Limondjian, a pianist herself, took her vacation and a leave from her job at the Met the summer of 1964. At the invitation of Frank Salomon, a codirector at Marlboro, she spent the summer helping out with the business end of things and she watched as the quartet formed. She remembers Janet Soyer showing her two pictures, mounted on velvet in oval Victorian frames; one was the face of Rudolf Serkin, and was titled "The Mother of the Guarneri"; the other was the face of Sasha Schneider, and was titled "The Father of the Guarneri."

At the end of the summer, she returned to New York and her job, singing the quartet's praises. The Budapest Quartet, which had had a sold-out series at the Metropolitan Museum for many years, had retired, and Miss Limondjian persuaded Dr. Kolodney to engage the Guarneri to succeed the Budapest. She says, "The audiences were 'fixed' on the Budapest, and it took a while for the Guarneri to catch on. But when they did, the demand for tickets was so great that I finally took my life in my hands and arranged for stage seating. Everyone was against it—the insurance company, management, the fire department. To reassure management that audience members would not be falling off the stage, I hired extra ushers. Three stood at each side of the auditorium, near the stage. They would presumably catch anyone who fell off." She adds, "The Guarneri has played for us every year since. They began their 'Guarneri & Friends' series at Alice Tully Hall in 1975. Eventually they played at the Frick Collection, Washington Irving High School, Rockefeller University, and, of course, they have a series at the Y. They defer to us, though, when they are choosing their programs. They try not to play the same quartet in the city twice in one season."

In 1975, Bill Lockwood, who is in charge of Lincoln Center's Great Performances series and the Mostly Mozart summer festival concerts, thought it was high time he got the Guarneri over to the West Side. Five years earlier, Charles Wadsworth had started his Chamber Music Society of Lincoln Center series, which included quartets, but specialized in offering assorted chamber works that the public would probably be hearing for the first time. Lockwood, who had invited the Guarneri to perform on the Mostly Mozart series in 1966, when they were only a year old ("They looked thunderstruck at the size of the audience—over two thousand people"), offered them the opportunity to play with guests of their choice, an offer they seized upon almost with glee. As with the Chamber Music Society series, the concerts have become so popular that each is played two nights in a row, and if the men had the time, they could easily fill the hall a third and fourth time.

The Guarneri took a tremendous financial risk when they became a quartet. In 1965, a string quartet did not command a fee, or enough concerts, to ensure a decent livelihood. And Steinhardt says, "We were all totally committed. We agreed to do nothing but play quartets. No free-lancing, special solo concerts." The Soyers, who gave up lucrative television-show jobs and jingle-recording work, moved to New Jersey. They didn't imagine they would ever again be able to afford to live in New York City. Lockwood feels that the Guarneri not only inherited the Budapest's mantle, but broke ground for new quartets, like the Cleveland, the Tokyo, the Vermeer, the Concord, enabling them to make a good living at what was no longer considered esoteric music. In the sixteen years since Mostly Mozart's inception, the ticket demand has shifted from orchestra concerts to chamber music. All concerts are sold out, but now the chamber-music tickets are the first to go. Lockwood and Wadsworth work closely together to avoid repertoire repetition: if both groups schedule the "Trout" Quintet, for instance, they make sure it's not performed twice in the same month.

Harry Beall tries to arrange the Guarneri's itinerary so that they will be away from home only for short periods—even if it means making two or three trips to the West Coast instead of one—and will have enough days off to keep them from killing themselves with overwork. In the two and a half months after their first concert of the 1977–78 season, at the

Ninety-second Street Y.M.–Y.W.H.A., they played in Middletown, Connecticut; Buffalo, New York; Huntington Woods, Michigan; St. Paul, Minnesota; Cleveland, Ohio; Old Westbury, New York; College Park, Maryland; Ithaca, New York; Binghamton, New York; Louisville, Kentucky; Decatur, Georgia; Birmingham, Alabama; Missoula, Montana; Portland, Oregon; Los Angeles, Stanford, Oakland, and Berkeley, California; Lawrence, Kansas; Buffalo again; Boston, Massachusetts—with three New York City concerts interspersed along the way. On November 30 and December 1, they would give a "Guarneri & Friends" concert, and the whole week would be a backbreaker. They were all looking forward to December 6 and a week in the South. Only four concerts and one open rehearsal—practically a vacation. Steinhardt would take his family along.

The quartet had scheduled the Elgar Piano Quintet for their "Guarneri & Friends" concert. The year before, in Europe, Tree had spoken to the French pianist Jean-Bernard Pommier about doing the work. There aren't many piano quintets, and the Guarneri is always interested in a new one. The Elgar had not been played in New York in twenty-five years. The first rehearsal, on November 29—the day before the concert—was held in Tree's apartment. The work was in Pommier's repertoire, but the quartet was playing it that day for the first time. They read through the piece, and to their dismay, none of them liked it. (When a work is seldom played, there may be a reason.) They considered changing the program, but read through the piece again. This time, there were sections they found appealing, and they decided to go ahead with it.

Pommier was on his way out the door when Soyer stopped him and asked when he wanted to rehearse the Brahms Clarinet Trio, with Soyer and Harold Wright. It was news to the pianist that he was supposed to play that the next night too. He didn't know it—he'd never even heard it. He told Soyer he would look at the score, listen to a recording, and get in touch with him. Brahms makes great demands on pianists, to say the least, and it was short notice for a public performance, but Pommier called Soyer that night and told him he could do it, and they could go through it the next morning, after the Elgar. The quintet turned out to be a pleasant treat for the audience, and Harold Schonberg thanked the artists, in an article in the *Times,* for giving New York a chance to hear it after so many years.

On the second of December, the Guarneri did the second of six concerts at the Metropolitan Museum's Grace Rainey Rogers Auditorium devoted to the Beethoven cycle (which they perform frequently, and which the year before had been played by three different quartets in the city); on the third, they did the early Schubert, the Lutoslawski, and the Brahms at Washington Irving High School, where the audience booed the Lutoslawski vehemently (Steinhardt said, "They asked for it; they *got* it"); on the fourth, they did a different Beethoven program for the Performing Arts Society in Philadelphia. On the fifth, Steinhardt gave a solo recital in the same city, and Tree and Soyer taught at Curtis. All four arrived in Charleston, South Carolina, on the sixth for an evening concert and an open rehearsal the following morning, and the South was having a cold snap—the temperature dropping into the twenties.

~

The Guarneri, in effect, brought string-quartet music to Charleston, and they are loved and lionized there. Kay Maves, who always acts as chauffeur and entertainment chairman when they're in town, left a note for her husband, David, who is chairman of the Fine Arts Department and teaches music composition at the College of Charleston, saying, "Get in gear! They're here!" Mrs. Maves met four separate planes and deposited, individually, Soyer, Steinhardt, and Tree in one hotel and Dalley in another. (The first year the quartet played in Charleston, they arrived on the same plane and were met by not only Mrs. Maves but a television crew with cameras.) The quartet had a quiet dinner shortly before the concert, at which they played one from Column A, one from Column B, and one from Column C—Schumann, Borodin, and the early Schubert, which had become the beauty Steinhardt had always said it was, and which was also the most difficult thing on the program: sentiment and simplicity are not easy to bring off.

They went to a party afterward—except for Dalley, who went back to his hotel—and the hostess's effort to lead them to a separate room for food was defeated when the guests crowded around them to talk. (Post-concert receptions stopped being called "cookie-pushers" a few years ago, when hostesses discovered that musicians are usually famished after a concert. Mozart composed the music, performed it, and ate with the servants. Two centuries later, Kreisler was asked by a woman of wealth to play for dinner guests. He told her his fee would be five thousand dollars, which startled her and prompted her to say, "Of course, you understand you're not to mingle with the guests." "In that case," Kreisler said, "the fee will be three thousand." These days, people vie for the privilege of providing elaborate post-concert parties.)

The open rehearsal was held at ten in the morning in a sunny student lounge at the College of Charleston, with a slightly premature Christmas tree and a long table holding a coffee urn, plastic cups and plates, and pastries. There were more than a hundred people in the audience, some seated on the floor—one young girl close enough to Dalley to turn pages for him—others on folding chairs. Quartet playing is a constant striving for an elusive perfection, and though the Guarneri had planned during the rehearsal to go over the works they had played the night before, instead they read through pieces they might include in next year's program. They did a Webern, and Tree dismissed it for all of them when he said, "It's gray, it's dull. He must have got in with bad company—Schoenberg, Berg . . ." Next, they played a César Franck, and whereas they agreed that there were some interesting sections, it was too long, and in places stickily sentimental, and if they programmed it they would become bored with it before the season was even half over. Then they read through the Mendelssohn D Major—an intricate work, fresh as a mountain stream, with hints of triumph and joy—and they liked it, and so did the audience, which applauded for the first time. A definite possibility for next year.

After driving Steinhardt and Dalley to the airport—Steinhardt's family was waiting for him at Captiva, an island off the southwest coast of Florida, and Dalley was planning to visit relatives in Orlando—Mrs. Maves took Soyer and Tree to a food mart, an enclosed city block of stands featuring specialties of various nationalities. Tree went directly to a seafood stand for she-crab soup—a Charleston specialty—and pecan pie. Soyer circled the area, took his time, and settled for a Greek *gyro*—mounds of thinly sliced, garlicky pressed beef and lamb on pita bread. So garlicky that Soyer said, "John and Arnold aren't going to appreciate this tomorrow night."

A tennis game had been arranged for Tree with the pro at the Seabrook Island Tennis Club, a private club on an island south of Charleston, and after lunch Mrs. Maves drove Soyer and Tree there. At the gate, there was a guard in a booth, and when she handed him a pass and said, "Mr. Tree has a reservation," Soyer, who was sitting next to her, and who was under the illusion that they were being taken to the Arab-owned island, Kiawa, also south of Charleston, leaned over and shouted, "Applebaum! Applebaum! Are you *meshuge?*" Tree was the first to arrive at the courts, and when the pro showed up he looked both nonchalant and annoyed. A viola player, of all things. Mrs. Maves drove Soyer to the beach clubhouse, which overlooked the water, and while he jogged up and down the beach she had some coffee and tried to get warm. When Soyer returned, they sat and talked for a while, Soyer studying the water and the bird life, and pointing out different birds to her. By the time they got back to the tennis courts, Tree was waiting, pink with pleasure. He had beaten the pro. He said, "I couldn't do it twice, I'm sure. I think I caught him off guard." In his excitement, Tree left his coat behind.

Later, after a break at their hotel for a shower, Mrs. Maves took them to a seafood restaurant, where her husband and two couples from the college Fine Arts Department were waiting, and where Tree and Soyer had enough seafood to keep them happy for a long time: crab legs in parsley and garlic sauce; red snapper buried in oysters and shrimp; a house salad almost defeated by crabmeat. Soyer, who is a natural raconteur and a joketeller, went through his repertoire, which varies from week to week. Many of the jokes are ethnic, and he tells them with roiling vowels and Catskill inflections, causing his listeners to laugh so hard at the delivery that they often miss the punch line. At midnight, after everyone had had a turn at trying to stack the four wine-bottle corks that had accumulated, Mrs. Maves made her final trip to the hotel. Her husband put his bike in the back of the station wagon and sat next to Tree. He told him he would pick them up in the morning and drive them to the airport. Tree and Soyer showed no signs of fatigue, but Mrs. Maves's eyes were at half mast.

The next morning on the way to the airport, David Maves ran out of gas. Soyer, drumming his fingers on the dashboard, said, "This is it. This will be a first. We're going to miss the plane." But Maves got out, vaulted over an approach rail to the throughway, ran a hundred yards to a Shell station, returned in minutes with a can of gas, and got them to the plane on time.

In Miami, Tree and Soyer were met by Victor Stern, a boyhood friend of Soyer's who was first violist in the Miami Philharmonic for twenty-five years and teaches at the University of Miami. With him was a tall Korean cellist, in Florida on a student's visa—a young man whose intense admiration of the quartet members suggested that it took will power for him to refrain from genuflecting. When Tree and Soyer checked into the hotel, the clerk asked if they would like connecting rooms. Tree said, "Lord, no. Separate floors, if possible," and Soyer said, "Separate buildings, if you have two."

The concert that night was given in a vast building that announced itself, in giant red neon letters, to be the Dade County Auditorium. It would be like playing in a football stadium. Steinhardt and Dalley were backstage when Soyer and Tree arrived. Steinhardt, who had forgotten his tie, borrowed one from a Cuban cellist, Manuel Capote, another friend of Soyer's who plays in the Miami Philharmonic. The audience was treated to the Lutoslawski, and Stern, eavesdropping at intermission, discovered that most of the people there —an assortment of the retired and an equal number of young people—liked the piece, thought it had humor in it. Some heard birdcalls, and others swarms of bees.

Backstage after the concert, Tree saw Steinhardt's uncle and aunt, who had recently moved to Florida from New Jersey. Tree hugged Steinhardt's aunt and kissed her on both cheeks and said, "Where's the cake?" Soyer laughed, and on

75

the way to the car he told Stern that she had once brought a cake backstage after a concert in Brooklyn, but she forgot forks, plates, a knife. "We ate it with our bare hands." Tree followed with Capote and the Korean fan and told Soyer that Capote was taking them to a restaurant that had the best Cuban food in town—white-bean soup, garlicky shrimp, Cuban beer. (Steinhardt was going back to Captiva, and Dalley to Orlando.) The restaurant was a small place, family-owned and family-run. Tree tasted the soup and rolled his eyes. Soyer tasted the shrimp, pronounced it delicious, and said, "Poor John, poor Arnold." Before leaving, Soyer studied a bullfight poster on the wall. He said to the owner, "Isn't that Manolete? His last fight?" The owner said it was, and on the way to the car Soyer told Stern about another bullfighter, Juan Belmonte. "Someone asked him what he did to prepare for a fight. He said, 'The bull weighs three thousand pounds and I weigh a hundred and thirty. I smoke cigars and pray. What the hell do you think I do?'"

Soyer had originally planned to stay in Winter Park and then Sarasota, where the next two concerts would be held. Instead, he changed his plane ticket the following morning and went to Tampa with Tree, who was planning to stay in Tampa and drive to the next two concerts. Bill Steckler was flying down to Tampa to play tennis with Tree. While Soyer was having his ticket changed, Tree, who has said that sometimes he feels more like a foot soldier than like a musician, took a pop-top can of V-8 juice out of his tennis case and drank it.

In the Tampa terminal, Soyer got to a car rental counter first. Tree's son had put zigzags of masking tape all over his father's luggage, for easy identification, but somehow it always seemed to be the last one coming out of the carrousel. Soyer went to Hertz and Tree to Avis. Bill Steckler was already at the motel when Tree and Soyer arrived. Tree was looking forward to a lot of tennis; there were courts adjoining the motel they all stayed in. Also, it was Friday, and they would be free until Sunday afternoon and the Rollins College concert in Winter Park. But Florida was having a cold snap, too—it was thirty-eight—and it was beginning to seem more like a wave than a snap. Friday afternoon Steckler and Tree played tennis, and before dinner all three practiced. (Steckler takes his violin with him wherever he goes. It's a Guarneri, more valuable than the instruments Steinhardt, Dalley, and Tree play.)

On Saturday, Soyer had breakfast in the motel restaurant with a former pupil, now a housewife but still playing, and lunch with another, Madalena Marx, a lovely Brazilian girl with long brown hair, who was in the Tampa Symphony. She was also in a piano trio, and she told Soyer the group was having personality problems—no one could take even minimal criticism. Soyer said, "It's an attitude none of you can afford—a destructive luxury. We learned that long ago." In the afternoon, Soyer had pictures taken for a new passport— his had expired—and he did some Christmas shopping. He says he married Janet so he could have a Christmas tree. Sunny, cold Florida was full of red tinsel Christmas trees—in Miami, they were topped with gold stars of David—and Madalena Marx had said, "At least the season is not depressing here. It just doesn't exist."

Saturday night they had dinner in Tarpon Springs, twenty miles from Tampa. A small village that calls itself the sponge capital of the world, it has a harbor filled with boats for the sponge hauls, and a string of small Greek restaurants that serve the kind of food that appeals to the quartet—authentic and non-American. Before they left Tarpon Springs, Steckler, who had been eyeing sidewalk stalls with sponges for sale, succumbed and bought an enormous one. Soyer looked at it and said, "It's too big for a car. Do you drive a bus?"

Tree and Steckler had played tennis most of Saturday, and Sunday morning they were out on the courts again. Steckler couldn't accept being beaten by Tree. He kept shaking his head, and he said to Soyer, "His form is odd. I've had lessons and I've played all my life, but no matter where I hit the ball, he returns it. And he has those damn strong legs."

Tree likes to get to a concert town early, with time for a leisurely meal and a chance to warm up. The Winter Park concert was scheduled for four in the afternoon, and the three, Steckler driving, left Tampa at noon. They'd been told the trip should take about two hours. Madalena had called Soyer and invited them all to dinner that night; she promised the Brazilian national dish, *feijoada completa.* She had made it for the Soyers in New York, and Soyer told Tree and Steckler, "You're in for a big treat." On the way to the car, Soyer found a flowered silk tie in the motel parking lot. He picked it up, examined it, and said, "I think I'll wear this today."

In the car, Steckler, who had a secret yearning that the Guarneri would let him sit in for Dalley just once, at a rehearsal—just one movement of anything—told Soyer and Tree that he'd had a funny dream the night before. "I dreamed that Harry booked you for two hundred and thirty-nine concerts, John got sick, and I sat in for him. I was so bad that the three of you picked me up and tossed me into the audience." Soyer said, "That's not a funny dream. On all three counts, it's a nightmare." (Perhaps the dream was prompted by an incident that happened before a Grace Rainey Rogers concert in the fall—the quartet was doing the Beethoven cycle this season. Steckler went, and he had his violin with him. He met Soyer outside the auditorium and stopped to talk. An amateur-musician friend of Steckler's arrived, and Steckler introduced him to Soyer. Soyer, deadpan, told the man that Dalley was sick and Steckler would take his place that night. Steckler says the word spread like wildfire, and when the quartet, including Dalley, came onstage, sighs of relief could be heard in the audience.)

Table-flat Florida, with acres of orange trees, their burdened branches burgeoning with vulgar oversize fruit, was beginning to get to them. Tree, rather aggressively, had asked three mornings in a row for fresh orange juice, knowing in advance what the answer would be: "We only have frozen." There are no directional landmarks for the newcomer driving from one town to another, just fast-food restaurants which all resemble one another, and all those oranges. Steckler got lost several times (he was beginning to think he'd been invited down to drive) and when they finally arrived in Winter Park —a pedestrian told them they were there; there was no sign —they stopped at a McDonald's for hamburgers. Soyer looked disgusted and muttered, "Dreck, dreck." Back in the car, he picked up Steckler's sponge and said, "We should have stayed in the car and eaten this."

Steinhardt, too, had been misinformed about how long it would take him to get to Winter Park, and he arrived at Rollins College on the dot of four. Like the others, he tries to get to a concert early and warm up, and he was trembling when he took his violin out of the case. Tree had told Soyer and Steckler that the program was all Beethoven, but the ushers were handing out programs that listed Beethoven, Schumann, and Debussy. Steckler, in the audience, glanced at the program and slipped backstage to alert Tree, who was unnerved but grateful. (In all the years they have played together, they have had only three program mishaps. Once, at Vassar, Soyer was poised for the stormy, dramatic opening bars of the Beethoven Opus 95. Instead, the others began with the serene, contemplative Beethoven Opus 18, No. 3. Soyer looked stunned. Then he raised his hand and commanded, "Stop!" He stood up, walked to the edge of the stage, and asked a woman in the front row if he could see her program. He glanced at it, turned to the others, and said triumphantly, "You guys are all wrong. We're playing Opus 95." Another time, Dalley had the wrong part. He left the stage and returned carrying the correct music on his head; the audience laughed. And in Miami, for reasons no one can remember, Tree, who is in charge of programs, had misinformed the others, and they had all brought the wrong music. Soyer announced the change to the audience, and he was loudly booed.)

The six Beethoven Opus 18 quartets, which represent his early period, are tricky works to begin a program with. Beethoven's sixteen quartets are considered the heart of quartet literature, and the early ones show an exquisite, controlled mastery of the form. The middle-period works reveal a branching out, a more profound understanding of the form, the instruments, and what the composer could say through them. The late Beethovens, composed when he could no longer hear, expose the soul of a man obsessed with the tortures of his life yet buoyed by the beauty of music. The Opus 18's, lighter in content than later works, are technically the most difficult to play, according to Tree—especially the 18 No. 2, the first work on the program in Winter Park. Tree says it's Beethoven's happiest piece; there isn't even a token slow movement. The Guarneri got off to a rocky start. Steinhardt flubbed a few notes in the beginning but warmed up as he went along. The Debussy which ended the program was stunning in every respect. Between repeated bows in response to the applause for the Debussy,

Steinhardt, in the wings, practiced a passage in the piece that hadn't pleased him.

Backstage, Soyer asked Dalley how the weather was in Orlando. Dalley said, "I didn't stay there. I flew home and peeled the linoleum off the kitchen floor. The wood looked pretty good, so I sanded the floor."

Steinhardt didn't bother changing clothes. He picked up his violin and sprinted out the door. He had a four-and-a-half-hour drive ahead of him. Tree called out, "See you in Sarasota," and Steinhardt stopped, smiled, and said, "I forgot to tell you. I resign."

In the parking lot, Soyer told Steckler and Tree that the found tie had special properties, that he'd rubbed it on his bow and played perfectly a spot in the Beethoven that he'd been flubbing for years. Steckler suggested that he have it insured by Lloyd's of London, and Soyer said, "That's a good idea."

Madalena had cooked the dinner in the apartment of friends, a couple, both of whom played in the Tampa Symphony. Tree said the *feijoada completa* was worth the long wait. Madalena's friends, in addition to playing in Tampa, do a short season in Mexico, another in North Carolina, and in the summer they coach at an amateur chamber-music camp in Vermont. Tree and Soyer were interested in everything they had to say about their musical experiences, and driving back to the motel, Soyer said, "They're working their tails off, and they probably make less than migrant fruit-pickers. They probably can't afford to have a baby. What a world."

The Southern cold snap continued, and Tree, who had intended to buy another coat somewhere along the line, never got around to it. On the drive to Sarasota Monday afternoon, he looked feverish, and he coughed steadily all the way, but during the concert that evening he did not play like a man who should be home in bed, and he didn't cough once.

Sarasota has a large community of music lovers, and it is proud of its Performing Arts Hall—designed by William Wesley Peters, of the Frank Lloyd Wright Foundation, a few years after Wright's death, with the color chosen by his widow. She picked purple—all purple. Purple everywhere. Soyer calls it the Purple Cow. (Actually, at night, artfully lighted, it looks mauve and very beautiful against the darker sky.) David Cohen, who studied violin for two years at Curtis and is a friend of the quartet, was mayor of Sarasota in 1964, when the bond issue for the arts hall was passed, and he was a strong force behind its passage. Cohen had arranged a buffet dinner for the quartet and friends at the Hyatt House, down the road, and it was the final fete of their seven-day "vacation," during which Steinhardt had driven over a thousand miles and Tree and Soyer over five hundred. The next morning, Soyer caught an eight-o'clock plane home, and Steckler and Tree, the latter feverish and miserable, followed two hours later.

～

The quartet likes the holiday season in December. They get to spend time with their families and see friends, and they do a number of concerts in the city. Also, they have a chance to unwind before their annual European tour. If the quartet's American tour looks unreasonable, their 1978 European tour looked insane: twelve concerts in fourteen days, with, at first glance, an opulent forty-eight free hours, though less opulent at second glance, since they would fall between Helsinki and Naples. They all say now that they had a marvelous time in Europe. (Tree likes European audiences. With rare exceptions, they are so enthusiastic that they seem almost dangerous, with their rhythmic clapping, stamping, and shouting. He says they play several encores and then run for their lives.) One of the highlights was the concert in Kuopio, Finland. The Finnish government has a policy of providing music for the hinterland, and the day after playing in Helsinki the quartet gave a concert in Kuopio, an hour's flight from the capital. There was no auditorium in the village, and they played in a church. It was hard to be serious. They sat in the choir loft, which was to the right of the audience and half a story above it, forcing the audience to listen with their heads turned at a forty-five-degree angle and tilted up, too, to enable them to see the musicians.

Eight of the quartet's forty-eight free hours were lost when the plane to Naples was delayed. In a number of places, Steinhardt's luggage never caught up with him, and he played in street clothes. (Violinists and violists have zippered canvas covers for their hard cases. The covers serve two purposes: they protect the expensive hard cases, and the zippers preclude a case's popping open if the clasps aren't properly latched. Steinhardt's luck with luggage has been so bad that he had a leather outer cover made to order in a sandal shop, with an extra pocket for music, and on long trips he stuffs in as much clean underwear as it will hold.) In Berlin, their path crossed that of the Amadeus, who had played the night before the Guarneri. Tree says, "A Berlin paper had a story about us headed 'Two Jewel Quartets in Berlin.' Not too many years ago, it would have said 'Two Jew Quartets . . .' " They're all good friends, and after the Guarneri concert a dinner party in a private home was held to honor both quartets.

In London, the night after Naples and the last stop, Soyer was momentarily jolted when a man greeted him warmly backstage; then Soyer realized that they'd met in New Zealand. He would have remembered him there. Tree says, "We think we're the only ones who travel. Everyone else should stay *put,* or it just confuses us."

On January 27, they gave the third of their Grace Rainey Rogers Beethoven concerts. Soyer played Casals' cello that night, and he clearly enjoyed it. He lightly flirted with difficult phrases, articulated nuances, and his excitement was contagious to the others. Not only were people in the Grace Rainey Rogers audience, normally almost chillingly subdued, standing and shouting "Bravo!" but some were whistling as well. The quartet had rehearsed that morning at Dalley's, and after the rehearsal Steinhardt—who had driven to New Jersey from his country house in upstate New York, near Tanglewood, that morning—and Tree played tennis for two hours on an indoor court near Yankee Stadium.

All up and down Fifth Avenue, there are friends of the quartet's who honor them with parties after their Grace Rainey Rogers concerts. This night, it was Mr. and Mrs. Irving Moskovitz, who live across from the Met in an apartment that, at first glance, is a miniature Louvre. Steinhardt, wearing a down jacket with satchel-size pockets over his black suit, greeted Mrs. Moskovitz warmly and said, "I love presents! Michael said we each get to take a painting home." Champagne was chilling in silver ice buckets, and there was a bar for pre-dinner drinks, but Steinhardt and Tree sent two maids scurrying. Steinhardt asked for hot tea and Tree requested orange juice. The apartment was filled with the quartet's friends and with friends of the Moskovitzes, and a large number of them were gathered as close as they could get to Soyer, who was telling jokes. A buffet dinner was served, and the hostess, knowing the Guarneri's enthusiasm for desserts, had provided three cakes, a platter of pastries, fresh fruit, and ice cream. Steinhardt was pleased to find Shmuel Ashkenasi at the party, and at twelve-thirty he went off with Ashkenasi to an all-night tennis court for two more hours of tennis. Ashkenasi, who had not driven from upstate New York, or rehearsed, or performed, kept muttering, "This is crazy. This will ruin me."

On February 1, the Guarneri played a new quartet by Vittorio Rieti with the Musica Aeterna Orchestra. The work was commissioned by Frederic Waldman, the orchestra's conductor. Works for quartet and orchestra are rare—possibly because the orchestra tends to engulf a quartet—and Waldman also had the quartet play the Elgar Introduction and Allegro. Usually, the principal players in an orchestra take the solo parts, and doing the Elgar was a slight embarrassment to the Guarneri, who felt the orchestra's principals, all friends of theirs, could do very well by the music. At rehearsal, the four sat in a diagonal row to the left of the podium, looking like four birds on a telephone wire, but they couldn't see or hear each other, and if they sat in regular formation Tree and Soyer wouldn't be able to see the conductor. At the concert, they sat in a semicircle, a solution only partly satisfactory to everyone. They looked splendid in white tie and tails. That was the customary stage dress for the quartet's first ten years, but one night on tour, playing in a college town, Tree noticed an audience of beads, beards, and bare feet, and they switched to dark suits. After the Elgar and the Rieti, Waldman conducted a piece for woodwinds and brass, and backstage the quartet rehearsed a Mozart they would be doing in Toronto two nights later. At a party after the concert, Steinhardt said, "I may not have played pretty, but I played *loud.*"

After that, the Guarneri went to Toronto, Montreal, Fort Wayne, Houston, Fresno, Berkeley, Pasadena, and La Jolla, with intermittent stops in New York, and in the middle of March they did four concerts with the Long Island Symphony Orchestra, conducted by Seymour Lipkin, originally a concert pianist. Tree says that when an instrumentalist turns to conducting, it's a loss to the music world, and in Lipkin's case, the loss was tremendous.

The Guarneri loves variety in music, and for these concerts, played in four different cities, they split up and did concertos: Tree and Dalley the Mozart Sinfonia Concertante in E-Flat Major for Violin and Viola; Soyer, Steinhardt, and Lipkin the Beethoven Triple Concerto; and Soyer and Steinhardt the Brahms Double Concerto. The Beethoven isn't performed very often; the expense of getting three soloists equal to the demanding parts is prohibitive. The cello solo in particular is a terror, and Janet Soyer reported to a friend at the first concert that while her husband was practicing his part he kept saying, "This is for shit!" Few composers have asked a cellist to play light, rapid pianistic passages that high up on the fingerboard. At a question period before the concert at Huntington, designed to give the audience a chance to get acquainted with the artists, Peter Leonard, Lipkin's assistant, who would conduct the Beethoven, asked Steinhardt and Tree to tell the audience something about the music they were going to play. (Lipkin and Soyer were backstage, practicing; Dalley had not yet arrived.) Steinhardt bent over and said into the microphone, "If Beethoven were alive today, every cellist who has ever attempted this piece would punch him in the nose."

The Mozart was played with such beauty and grace and mutual understanding that someone in the audience was heard to say, "Maybe it should always be played by quartet members." For the Beethoven, Soyer sat on a high platform, so he could see Lipkin and the conductor, and he looked uncharacteristically vulnerable. During the orchestral introduction in the Brahms, which Lipkin conducted, Steinhardt, head bowed, violin tucked under his right arm, stood back from the

86

music. Lotte Lehmann once advised a student during a master class not to be rigid, but to "step into the music." And this Steinhardt did. Standing, in white tie and tails, he is a wondrously dramatic figure. He and Soyer were swarmed by autograph seekers after the concert. (Tree and Dalley left after the Mozart.) Steinhardt's parents, who live in Los Angeles, were in New York for a visit, and they were there. At a post-concert dinner party in a restaurant, a middle-aged woman came up to Steinhardt and said, "Forgive me for interrupting you. I did want to tell you that I have heard many great violinists in my life, and no one gave me the pleasure you did tonight." Steinhardt looked openly pleased, and he thanked her. After she had left, his mother said, "Don't let it go to your head."

Steinhardt drove his parents and Peter Leonard and his wife, Paula, back to the city. In the car, Steinhardt talked about the Beethoven. He said, "Dave played a phrase so very beautifully, and I had the same phrase coming up. I thought, 'I'm going to have to do it especially well to sound the way Dave does,' and I did my best, and at the end of the phrase I glanced down and noticed a woman in the front row yawning so mightily I could see all her dental work." Even though he'd made the trip to Huntington for rehearsals, he was not familiar with the area, and he got lost several times. It was after three when he reached the city, and he stopped to let out the Leonards, who had slept most of the way. Steinhardt got out to open the trunk, which held Leonard's garment bag, and said goodnaturedly, "I'm going to have a bunch of keys made for this trunk and give them to my friends." It was a bitter cold, windy night, and Leonard asked, "Arnold, where do you get the energy? How do you keep it up?" Steinhardt said with a smile, "Well, it's my whole life. I might as well enjoy it."

~

On April 2, the Guarneri flew to the Midwest for a five-day, four-state tour. The first stop was the University of Iowa, in Iowa City, and the only way to get there was via Chicago and Cedar Rapids, twenty miles from Iowa City. Steinhardt and Tree booked a TWA flight out of La Guardia, and Soyer, who had shared a cab to the airport with them, dropped them off and went on to American Airlines. According to Soyer, TWA has made both him *and* his cello fly first class, and Delta has required a first-class ticket for the cello—half fare in both cases. Soyer says it galls him. As a matter of fact, since the others share in the cost, it galls them, too. Once, when Soyer and Tree were on the same Delta plane, Tree walked up to first class and asked a stewardess for the cello's dessert. She said there was no meal on board for the instrument. (Another time, when they were all on standby, "Mr. Cello" was the first to be called for a seat.) In the airport, Steinhardt bought two paperbacks for plane reading—Dickens's "Hard Times" and Graham Greene's "The Power and the Glory." All four read a great deal on planes, and their choices are eclectic. A Mark Twain specialist in one university town was surprised to discover that Soyer had read everything Twain had written.

The men assumed that on a morning flight to Chicago breakfast would be served. Instead, they each got a silver-dollar-size pastry and coffee. Tree and Steinhardt were sitting together, and Tree said, "I sat with a man on a plane recently who had phoned ahead and requested a kosher meal. You should have seen what *he* got. Fresh orange juice, three pastries, with butter. I'm going to start doing that, and if my cheeks get pinker and my playing improves, I suggest we all do it." They would have a free day between Milwaukee and Oxford, Ohio, and Steinhardt, who was reading *Time,* showed Tree an article about a German Impressionist show currently in Chicago. Steinhardt said, "I think I'll go to that on my day off." Each has a discerning eye and the beginning of a fine art collection. (Soyer had told them in the cab that on *his* day off he was going to go to a movie. Instead, he heard the Chicago Symphony.)

Dalley, who had taken a plane out of Newark, was at the gate for the one-thirty flight, on Ozark Air Lines, to Cedar Rapids. It was the first time that season that all four were on the same plane. He said he was almost sure he'd left all his music behind; he couldn't remember packing it. Soyer said, "I hope you did. We can probably borrow everything from a library but the Lutoslawski, and I don't care if we never play that piece again."

Iowa City rolled out the red carpet all the way to Cedar Rapids. James Wockenfuss, the director of cultural events at the university, met the plane, along with a music student: two cars, so no one would be crowded. Wockenfuss drove his own car, and the student drove one with "The University of Iowa" emblazoned in white letters on both front doors. Wockenfuss, a prematurely gray, energetic man, in a brown suede jacket, asked the Guarneri for their luggage tickets and said that he and the student would see to it that everything was present and accounted for. Soyer's and Dalley's bags were not on the plane, and neither was the case Tree carries his tennis equipment in. Wockenfuss checked with the Ozark clerk and reported that the bags would be on a plane arriving at seven in the evening. The student would pick up the luggage and bring it directly to the auditorium, where Soyer and Dalley could change. *If* Dalley had left his music at home, the program scheduled for that night—Schumann, Beethoven, Debussy— was sure to be in the repertoire of the Stradivari Quartet, in residence at the university and in town at the moment. (As it turned out, Dalley *had* packed his music.)

By the time they reached the motel they would stay in—

the Highlander—it was three o'clock. They all have what Beall calls "business assignments," and Steinhardt supposedly handles domestic travel. He never does, except in the Midwest, where Tree insists that he take charge of Tree's and his own accommodations. Steinhardt procrastinates, and often the two end up in the airport on standby and then in a fleabag hotel, but still Tree persists. The Highlander desk clerk had Tree and Steinhardt assigned to adjoining rooms, and Tree said, "Damn it, Arnold, I wish you would tell your travel agent to stop doing this," and he added to the clerk, "I don't want to be on the same floor with *any* of them." There was a reason for his annoyance. He practices as much as he can on tour, so that when he's home he'll have more free time to spend with his family, and he wanted privacy. Dalley studied the registration form—name, address, firm. He said, "I'm middle-aged, but I'm still firm." While he filled it out, he said, "Lord, I get sick of doing this. I'm going to have a rubber stamp made with all the pertinent information on it."

They hadn't eaten much all day, and they were hungry, but the motel dining room was closed. Wockenfuss drove Soyer, Steinhardt, and Tree to a Howard Johnson's for lunch. Dalley used room service. A party was planned for after the concert, and Soyer, studying the menu, said, "Is it going to be one of those carrot-stick things?" Wockenfuss assured him that a caterer would provide ample food for the dinner party, which was to be at his home. There are a number of gourmet cooks among faculty wives in Iowa City, including Mrs. Wockenfuss, and no first-rate restaurants, but none of the wives wanted to miss the concert. (In other communities, if the quartet is appearing for the second time, something is always planned for them. It could be a potluck supper, to which a number of chamber-music enthusiasts contribute a dish, or, if money is not an issue, a sit-down dinner in a restaurant. In

Missoula, Montana, one man—a local journalist, overjoyed by a string-quartet concert instead of the usual rock or bop—rented a whole mountaintop restaurant and reviewed the concert, too. Only Soyer and Steinhardt went to the party, but that did not keep the host from heading his review "The Greatest String Quartet in the World.")

It was cold in Iowa too, but after eating, Soyer, Steinhardt, and Tree decided to walk back to the motel, for the exercise, and they set off across a windswept Willa Cather prairie, bisected by a four-lane throughway, shoulders hunched against the wind. Heading for the same place, they went in three different directions—Steinhardt straight ahead toward a gully, which he leaped over; Tree to the left, bypassing the gully; Soyer along the throughway and up the motel's driveway.

Twenty-five years ago, the University of Iowa's School of Music was housed in a dark brick six-story building that at one time had served as the university's hospital. The campus was spread all over town, and to accommodate the postwar influx of GI's, Quonset huts popped up like mushrooms, giving Iowa City an oddly war-torn look. But in the sixties a program of revitalization was begun. A new art building went up, and seven years ago a music building was opened. The students—twenty-two thousand five hundred in number—made major contributions to both. In the past, their activities fee was fifty cents a semester, which paid for an occasional lecturer, the Minneapolis Symphony, and one or two other musical events —lumped together under the term "extracurricular," and primarily for students. The activities fee has since been increased to sixty-five dollars, eight of which have helped pay for the new auditorium. In exchange for their contribution, the students pay less than the public does for tickets to theater, dance, and music events, and they have first choice of seats. They also choose, through an elected committee that works with Wockenfuss, what the events will be, and Wockenfuss says that student interest in classical music has gone up thirty percent in the past six years. Also, the word "extracurricular" is no longer used. If a substitute term were to be picked, it should be "big business." The total expenditure for visiting performing artists was twenty thousand dollars in 1970. In 1977, box-office receipts came to four hundred and seventy-five thousand. The projection for 1980–81, when the Guarneri will give two concerts and play the Bartók cycle, is six hundred thousand dollars. Wockenfuss is proud of the new music building, which overlooks the Iowa River and has two auditoriums —Hancher Auditorium, which seats almost twenty-seven hundred, and Clapp Recital Hall, which seats seven hundred. Hancher, a wedge-shaped auditorium with traditional concert-hall colors—royal-red carpets and white walls—has wonderful acoustics. For all its space, there is a feeling of intimacy; people in the last row of the balcony feel included in what's happening onstage. The Guarneri had played in Iowa City the year before, and the audience numbered six hundred and fifty. For this concert, there were to be roughly fourteen hundred in the audience, and Wockenfuss said, "The next time they come, they'll fill the place."

A doctor who directs a six-hundred-calorie six-hundred-dollar-a-day health spa in southern California has scoffed at golf as an effective exercise. He was quoted in *The New York Times* as saying, "You don't burn any more calories playing golf than you do playing the cello." The doctor would be astonished at the amount of energy expended during a concert by the Guarneri. Even their entrance onstage is electrifying. They move quickly, easy with each other and the instruments they carry, which reflect the stage lights and gleam like jewels. They have tremendous presence, confidence. They are clearly looking forward to what they are about to do. The audience in Hancher Auditorium leaned back, relaxed, anticipating an evening of Schumann, Beethoven, and Debussy—the last played with such shimmering, delicate beauty that there was a moment's silence before the audience began applauding and shouting "Bravo!" A long queue of people who wanted to greet the artists formed outside the greenroom. A uniformed usher opened the door for the crowd when the quartet was ready to receive them. Tree was pleased and surprised at the sight of two students he had taught when the quartet was at Harpur College. After the room had emptied, Wockenfuss asked the four to sign their names in a book he keeps of signatures of all artists who appear there, and the names preceding theirs were impressive: Isaac Stern, Garrick Ohlsson, Beverly Sills, Joan Sutherland, Alicia de Larrocha, Vladimir Horowitz (for whom the chairman of the School of Music, Himie Voxman, relinquished his home; Voxman and his wife moved into a motel), Andrés Segovia, Arthur Rubinstein. The audience that night included people from fifty-two towns, some over a hundred miles away. People at the university are fond of this story: One afternoon, a Cadillac with California license plates and a uniformed driver pulled up to the Highlander, and an elderly couple got out and went in to register. The man asked the desk clerk if anything of interest was going on in town, and the desk clerk said, "The San Francisco Ballet is at Hancher Auditorium tonight." The woman looked blankly at her husband and said, "I thought you said we were in Iowa."

Wockenfuss drove Tree and Dalley to the party at his house, and on the way Tree said, "Oy, the way we played last year I'm surprised you asked us back. We were exhausted." Wockenfuss said it sounded good to him. What was wrong? Tree rolled his eyes and said, "Let's just call it loose ensemble."

Wockenfuss's living room, warmed by a fire blazing in the fireplace, was filled when the quartet arrived. Professor Voxman and his wife and the four members of the Stradivari and their wives—friends of the quartet—were there, and so was John Simms, the head of the Piano Department and a Curtis graduate. Simms's career had seemed to be ended when the fourth finger of his left hand was hit by a piece of shrapnel during the Second World War. He came to Iowa City to teach and to relearn the repertoire with fingerings that would favor the stiff one. But he liked teaching, and the Midwest, and he stayed on. He has recorded a substantial part of the sonata literature with the violinist Rafael Druian, and the week before he had played, with the university symphony, the Rachmaninoff Third Piano Concerto—a work that seems to belong to Horowitz. Many pianists avoid it, because it is so very difficult. Simms's performance, from all accounts, was a triumph. The catered dinner was a success: bœuf bourguignon, kept warm in a chafing dish; hot rolls in a basket; asparagus with hollandaise sauce; an enormous wooden salad bowl filled with a variety of tossed greens; a chocolate soufflé. A uniformed bartender helped the guests to red wine and made sure their glasses were never empty. The conversation between the two quartets was animated, and Simms had a long talk with Dalley, whose father is a friend of Simms's. At midnight, Steinhardt collapsed in a chair—a puppet with loose strings—and said, "I'm exhausted." The party gradually broke up.

The next morning, Tree and Steinhardt played tennis for two hours before the four caught a plane to St. Louis. Steinhardt, who was carrying in his wallet a devastatingly vicious review written by a California critic who had never liked the quartet ("They were worse than ever this year, if that's possible"), would have appreciated what Simms told his piano seminar the next day. He said, "I have rarely heard such musicianship, and never before from a string quartet. Their phrasing is breathtaking. There are no unwanted accents, and there is a freedom that is conceptual, that transcends bar lines. They have the secret of truly beautiful playing."

~

One of the Guarneri's first recordings was the Tchaikovsky Sextet, "Souvenir of Florence," with Sasha Schneider and Boris Kroyt from the Budapest as the guest artists. The Cobbett Cyclopedia Survey of Chamber Music calls the piece the feeblest of Tchaikovsky's works, though it includes it in the generalization that "the elegiac tendencies of Tchaikovsky's music are nowhere more evident than in his chamber works." The Guarneri recording was dropped from the Schwann catalogue for a brief period because there was no demand for it. As the fame of the quartet grew, the demand for their records increased, and the Tchaikovsky was reissued with a new, eye-catching jacket. Tree says people don't think of Tchaikovsky as a chamber-music composer and possibly many record buyers didn't know the sextet existed. It is rhapsodic, infectious, and the BBC used it throughout their "Anna Karenina" series, even when Anna and Vronsky were not in Florence. Russian pairs skaters would be wise to use it in competition—especially the last movement's second subject, which lends itself to the soaring movement only great skaters and eagles are capable of. Tree says, "We recorded it in Webster Hall, on the Lower East Side, with Max Wilcox in charge. At the lunch break, we'd all go to Rappaport's and gorge ourselves on borscht and blintzes. Afterward, the four of us felt leaden and logy, but Boris and Sasha, while we listened to the replays, danced around the studio—Russian folk dances. They waltzed around like great Russian bears, and it was a tremendous joy for all of us."

Wilcox also produced Arthur Rubinstein's records. Almost fanatic about his recordings, Rubinstein would always listen to a tape ready for release, often decide he didn't like it, and withhold permission for its release. One day in June 1965, Rubinstein came to RCA to hear a tape of his that RCA wanted to produce. Wilcox says, "After the session, we lit cigars—a sign that the tape pleased him. I told him there was something I wanted him to hear, and I put on a tape of the Guarneri playing the Mozart Quartet in F, K. 590. Rubinstein's wonderfully expressive face was rapt in attention. He began to exclaim about the freedom and power of the performance, the beautiful tone, the phrasing. He said he might be interested in doing a recording with them—possibly the Brahms Piano Quintet. I said I would arrange a meeting, but he began to back down. He said, 'We both know what you can do with tape, Max,' and he winked at me. Then I suggested that they get together and play, and see how they got along. He wouldn't be locked into a recording situation if he didn't like working with them. Rubinstein had given up his great Taj Mahal apartment on Park Avenue, and they all met in his hotel room, in the Drake. They got along famously."

Steinhardt says, "There were no clashes in musical ideas. I expected to be permanently awestruck, to not be able to forget it was Rubinstein I was playing with. But I discovered that he doesn't have the kind of personality that pushes you away, or makes you uncomfortable." Steinhardt adds, "When you're playing with a man of that stature, you tend to defer to him, though he never *demanded* that. As a matter of fact, there were several times when our ideas differed, and we would ask if he would mind doing, say, a certain phrase in another way. He was absolutely reasonable, and I was very relaxed with him."

Rubinstein was relaxed with them, too, and the following day they recorded the Brahms Quintet. It went so well that, over a celebration dinner at Lüchow's, Rubinstein said, "Let's record the Schumann Quintet tomorrow." After dinner, the quartet raced to Steinhardt's apartment to practice. Possibly Rubinstein practiced, too. He had played the quintet five years earlier, in the Library of Congress, with the Budapest. What Wilcox called "a historic collaboration" eventually recorded the major piano quartet and quintet repertoire.

Dalley says of the experience, "He's an intuitive player. We practiced as we went along, improved with each take." Soyer says, "He is, of course, a great artist. One fascinating thing about him: we'd make a take of a movement, and in his inimitable manner he'd put in a rubato here, a rubato there, and then we'd make another take and he'd have a whole new set of them. He seemed to pull them out of his pocket. An inexhaustible supply of these subtle things. He was like a colleague—cooperative, amiable—and he wasn't dogmatic. Things were always discussed, but it turned out that we agreed very much with the way he wanted to do things. His playing was stunningly beautiful. On very few occasions did we have any disagreement. A few things, perhaps. He was not a prima donna at all. It was very much chamber-music playing. I learned a lot from him; just listening to the man play was an educational experience."

Soyer adds, "I remember in particular recording the Brahms C Minor Quartet. Rubinstein said he was looking forward to the last movement. He'd played the piece just for fun with Casals, Ysaÿe, and the violist Lionel Turtis, and after the third movement, Ysaÿe always wanted to take a break for coffee, and Rubinstein claimed they never got around to finishing the piece." Dalley says, "It wasn't like a quartet session, when you can float along. We had to be on our toes every single minute. At the end of the day, I was pooped. I think he could have gone on forever. I envied him his incredible energy." Tree says it was fascinating to be able to watch Rubinstein at such close range. "Some of the best moments were listening to him reminisce. He'd just written his first book, and I think he was trying some of the material out on us. Also, he played for us, and, unfortunately, that was never recorded. He would sit at the piano and let his fingers drift. He'd play pieces for us—little-known things, excerpts from pieces he'd played years ago, vignettes from the Romantic literature. It was a lesson. I wish every young pianist could have the opportunity to hear him sit and dream at the keyboard."

The five men agreed to perform in public, at the Royal Festival Hall, in London; in the Théâtre Champs-Élysées, in Paris; and at the Grace Rainey Rogers Auditorium, in New York. In London, the largest hall of all, the demand for tickets was one that could never be met. (In New York, the final concert of the three coincided with the Metropolitan Museum's centennial; Hilde Limondjian placed a tiny ad in the *Times,* announcing the event. There was a stampede for tickets.) Royal Festival Hall was packed to the rafters. The stage was almost filled with extra seats, and people were sitting in the aisles. Soyer says, "Every musician within shouting distance was there: Menuhin, Barenboim, Jackie du Pres, Roger Ricci, hordes of people. And the BBC was broadcasting the concert. It was a *big* occasion. When we went onstage, Rubinstein was white as a sheet—frightened out of his mind. He was not accustomed to playing in public with music on the rack. He had glasses on, which he normally didn't wear onstage. Here he is, surrounded by four guys with instruments. He probably felt like he was in a cage. It was not his normal habitat." Tree later said that just before they went out, Rubinstein intimated to him that he suddenly realized a recording situation and a public performance were two distinctly different things. Soyer reminded Rubinstein that Arnold would give the cue to begin. The piece starts with the five playing the grand opening statement in unison. Tree, to Soyer's left, started to put his viola up, and when he moved, Rubinstein suddenly began to play. Four audible scrambled entrances followed. But after that initial fiasco, Rubinstein relaxed, and the evening was the triumph that everyone had anticipated.

In 1979, while the quartet was in the middle of a recording session, Rubinstein—who was at RCA to listen to a tape of his he was reluctant to have released—learned that they were in the building, and went to see them. He has very little vision left, and the first thing he said to them was: "I feel so silly, being ninety-two." Soyer says, "He reminisced about the times we played together, how we made music. 'Those were the good old days.' It was very touching." In 1980, Rubinstein's second book of memoirs was published. In it, he mentions the pleasure of recording with "the brilliant, young Guarneri," and he lists all the works they did, but he has nothing to say about the public performances.

~

These days, the Guarneri records every spring and fall—from four to eight days each time, depending on how many works RCA hopes to get out of them. They all agree that the sessions are grueling—from ten to five, with a brief lunch break. Quite a contrast from a concert, which lasts a little over two hours and causes the adrenaline to flow. Microphones are no substitute for an audience. The Guarneri records works they have played during the season, and at recording sessions they dismantle, overhaul, completely revamp a work they have played perhaps seventy or eighty times. Tree says, "In a recording, we try for subtleties that would be lost onstage. Also, a slight exaggeration, a ritard, an embellishment can be effective in a concert; on a record it could begin to annoy you half to death. A note a shade flat onstage is lost forever, or at least soon forgotten. It would be intolerable on a record." Some people feel they would rather have a "live" recording, defects and all, and Soyer says, "We would record live—if everyone else did. But the live recordings issued these days—Horowitz at Carnegie Hall, and so on—are only half-truths. Patchwork is always done, cleanup work, all blemishes removed. Even the old Budapest recordings—the ones done at the Y; you can hear trucks roaring down Lexington Avenue —were polished. Note-splicing techniques didn't exist then, but performers could do four and a half minutes of music over and over until they were satisfied." Dalley, succinct as usual, has said, "If an actor did on camera the same things he did onstage, the results would be ludicrous. The situation is parallel in recordings."

In May 1978, with the end of a season once more in sight, they spent two days recording the Haydn Opus 77, No. 2— it would be the flip side for the Opus 77, No. 1, which they had recorded the previous fall—and two days recording the Brahms A Minor. Peter Dellheim, their A & R man, hoped to get them to do all three Brahmses—an unusual move, since the Cleveland had already recorded them for RCA (but perhaps not unusual, considering the fact that in October 1949, the Schwann catalogue listed one recording for each of seven Beethoven quartets—six by the Budapest, one by the Busch Quartet—and now offers the record buyer a choice of ten different groups recording all sixteen Beethoven quartets). The Guarneri usually recorded in Studio A, on the fourth floor of a building on West Forty-fourth Street where RCA rents space, with Dellheim acting as producer and with Edwin Begley as engineer. There is a third man there, a technician who feeds tape into the machine and rewinds takes to be played back.

Dellheim, an attractive, rather puckish-looking man of fifty-one, appeared to be much younger. He had brown hair and wore horn-rimmed glasses, above which his eyebrows shot when he was feigning astonishment. He had a shadow of an accent from eleven childhood years spent in Germany, where he was born, and two years in England, where his family moved in 1938 and where he went to school. He played piano and spent three years at the Eastman School of Music, in Rochester, New York. He said, "At Eastman, I found out what my talents are: I know how to listen, and I have taste. And the nice thing is, I was able to find work that suited my talents. I have to keep the artists on the track, in focus, in the sense of doing an actual performance. Music has to flow —one note leading to another. It has to have vitality, which can easily be lost in the recording situation. The artists know those mikes are merciless. I work to encourage spontaneity; that's why I sometimes say very outrageous things to them. It's a privileged relationship.

"Early in my career, I produced a record of a celebrated international pianist doing the Liszt Sonata. When he came to the coda, he played it half as fast as it's supposed to be played. When we listened to the take, I kept looking at him, expecting him to say something. I even thought, 'Maybe he's playing it slowly to practice it.' On the second take, he did it again. I thought, 'Well, I've got to take the bull by the horns.' I said, 'Do you have a different edition from mine?' He said, 'Why do you ask?' and I said, 'The coda ought to go twice as fast as you're doing it, according to my edition.' He looked very surprised, and he said, 'You know, that place has always bothered me. And I didn't know why. I've been playing this piece for twenty years, and nobody ever said anything to me about it.'

"That gave me confidence. I have to get the attention of the artists I work with. I have to get them up. They have to feel excited, as if they were doing a live performance, and it's hard to do. Some of the things the quartet plays are terribly difficult. I feel the Guarneri is the greatest quartet in the world—there's a vibrant strength there; they bounce off each other all the time, stimulate each other—but I don't tell them that. And I don't dwell on it. I can't be overawed by the musicians I work with. I like the Guarneri's approach. They're four great guys—all different. They come in—Arnold says it's like a comic book: 'Zap! Wow! Bang!'—and at first they try to push each other, push me, until things get out of kilter. Usually, by Take 4 they settle down. They're kind to each other then—I don't mean grubbily kind, just enough so that it comes together—and when that happens it's magical. And it's so different from an actual performance, where no one is there to tell them what to do. There are different elements working, which are psychologically very important. At a concert, the audience is there because they want to be; they bought tickets. There's a kinetic energy floating around, and a visual element. It's not unlike watching an athletic event. The bodily movement engages part of you. If your eyes go up, your ears are going to go down a little. And you're not going to focus both equally. The point about records is you're using only your ears. When I record, I have to focus, too, and listen as if I were hearing something for the fiftieth time. Afterward, I'm terribly tired. I follow a score while the quartet plays. Some of the works are new to me, but if you know the grammar of music, which I do, familiarity isn't necessary. If I notice on the first take that there are certain bars that are very problematical, in terms of intonation or ensemble, then, as we go along, I'll mark those particular spots as to which take is good. If they play it right once, I know I've got it. But all the technology in the world can't produce a miracle for the performer. Sometimes the end result of a recording session is a stillbirth.''

Studio A is in two sections. The outer room, the control room, is quite long and fairly narrow. Begley sits at a panel of needles and knobs sizable enough to keep a Boeing 727 aloft. Dellheim sits to Begley's right, with the score on a desk in front of him. There is a microphone on his desk, and when he wants to speak to the musicians while they are performing in the studio he flicks a switch. To Dellheim's right are the machines that hold the tape; to Begley's left are two Dolby machines designed to improve the quality of the sound. Behind the two men are four chairs for the musicians when they come into the control room to listen to a playback. In front of the instrument panel are three leather armchairs and a window with a view of the recording studio—a vast wood-paneled room with an adjustable ceiling, which can be moved up or down, and which appeared that day to be about thirty feet high. Dellheim records the quartet on eight-track tape, using eight microphones. Four, placed three or four feet above the musicians, are on stands, bent in the middle, the mikes nodding over the instruments. Four other mikes, one in each corner, some eighteen feet high and looking like four giraffes in a desert, pick up the ambient sound.

Steinhardt was the first to arrive for the Brahms recording, and he went directly into the studio, unpacked his violin, sat down, and began practicing the Brahms. The last thing he'd done the day before was the Presto movement of the Haydn, in which he played fourteen hundred and three notes in four minutes and eleven seconds—seven complete takes and five aborted takes—and, elbow absolutely flying, he looked like a country fiddler at a hoedown. Today, Dellheim said, "Arnold, what did you have for breakfast? You sound so energetic." Steinhardt said cheerfully, "Riboflavin," and continued to practice. Dellheim said to Begley, "I'm going to have to wear him down a bit; he sounds a little hysterical."

Tree and Dalley arrived, by chance, together. The Budapest need not have cautioned the Guarneri about traveling together. On recording days, they seldom take the same elevator. There is only one, and the first to pack up and leave doesn't hold it for any stragglers.

Soyer was the last to arrive. A bus driver wouldn't let him on the bus with his cello—even though the bus wasn't full and Soyer offered the driver another token. It was raining, and cabs were scarce. RCA had recently reissued some old Flonzaley recordings on LPs, and Begley was listed on the record jacket as the engineer. Soyer teased him about it. He said, "Ed, I didn't know you'd been around so long—1904. You don't look that old. Tell me—on that first record, did you hold the needle and have a friend turn the record or was it the other way around?"

Begley, a pleasant gray-haired man, laughed and said, "I know which track is yours. You might as well turn around and go home. No one's going to hear a note out of you today."

Soyer helped himself to some coffee from a pot that is kept filled and hot as long as there is a musician around who might want some. There is a rather large first-aid kit attached to the wall near the door, and toward the end of a rough day it's not hard to imagine there being some use for that, too. Soyer went into the studio, unpacked his cello, and joined the others. Steinhardt said, "Let's play the first movement through once, before we start recording. Is that O.K., Peter?" Dellheim said,

"Yes, go ahead—it's a good idea. You're too steamed up right now anyway."

Brahms did not make sketches of his chamber works, as earlier composers did—much in the way an artist sketches on a canvas before beginning an oil painting. The four voices in a Brahms quartet are cat's-cradle interwoven, each too rich, too important for a simple sketch. Brahms's method of composing—textural, less linear than that of composers who preceded him—required that he virtually complete a composition before he knew whether or not it pleased him, and, to the dismay of many musicians, there is evidence that he destroyed almost twenty quartets before he died. His music tends to be impassioned, haunting, compelling, and hard to keep in check. Quartet-playing amateurs seem propelled into playing louder and louder, sometimes faster, until the music seems to be controlling them. Partway into the first movement, Tree had a lush solo. Brahms favored the viola and frequently gave that instrument something special to do. Steinhardt stopped playing and said, "Mike, you can wiggle your ass once on that, but not three times." They started again and finished the movement.

Dellheim flicked the switch and said, "I think you're ready. Can we start now?" Dalley answered, "We might as well," and Dellheim said, "Stand by, gentlemen, please. HRA 4-6651, Take 1."

They played the first movement without interruption, in nine minutes and twenty seconds, and after they finished they came in to listen to the replay. Soyer had heard no more than two minutes when he said, "Peter, you could blackmail us with this." Steinhardt sat relaxed, legs stretched out, looking boneless. Dalley listened intently, and Tree stood behind Dellheim and followed the score, occasionally pointing out a spot and saying something about it to Dellheim. Dellheim said, "Mike, you're swinging your body in wide arcs, and the sound is very uneven. Can you sit still?" Tree said, "Thanks. I'll try," and to Soyer, "Dave, I think you and I are being shortchanged. I hear too much violin." Dellheim agreed with Tree and said, "I don't want to move the mikes. They're well placed. If I move Dave's and Mike's closer to them, they'll be whacking them with their bows. Arnold and John, why don't you move your chairs back a couple of inches?" Dalley said, "I'd like to move back thirty feet," and Steinhardt said, "I'm sorry I practiced."

Soyer said, "Let's do it again," and they went back in and sat down. As is their habit, they immediately started noodling at different passages, practicing again. Dellheim cut in: "Stand by, please, gentlemen. HRA 4-6651, Take 2."

While they were playing, Begley said, "I hear a faint buzz —five seconds, intermittently." Dellheim heard it too, and using a phone on his desk, he called for help. Two engineers arrived within seconds, discussed various possibilities and ruled them out. Dellheim said, "Maybe I can edit around it."

The quartet finished Take 2 and came in to listen. Tree asked Dellheim for the time, and Dellheim said, "It's nine twenty-seven—seven seconds longer than the first one."

Tree said, "I had no idea the piece was so long. Is it going to fill two sides?"

Dellheim said, "The three Brahmses are often done on two records. Let's see where we're at when we get all three done."

Soyer stubbed out his cigarette and said, "Let's go."

When they were back inside, Dellheim flicked the switch and said, "All of you—those pizzicato chords are a mess. They're not together."

Soyer said, "Why don't you borrow them from the Cleveland?"

They were well into Take 3 when Steinhardt broke a string. Tree said, "Damn! That was a fantastic take." While Steinhardt was replacing the string, Tree said, "Peter, maybe you can use part of it."

At the beginning of Take 4, Soyer hit the mike with his bow. He stopped and said, "Ed, did I louse up the mike?" Begley checked the instrument panel and said, "No, it's O.K."

When Dellheim wants to make a strong point, instead of speaking through the mike he goes into the studio. At the end of Take 5, he went in.

Dalley muttered, "Oh-oh. Here comes Teacher."

Dellheim said, "If you want to do it that way, that's your business. To me it sounds absolutely gross. I can't feel the beat. You're pulling in all directions."

Steinhardt protested, "But the rhythm is two against three against four. It's like four guys tied in a huge gunnysack struggling every which way to get out." He flailed his long arms and legs wildly in all directions, miraculously managing not to knock his stand over or hit his mike.

Dellheim said, "Nevertheless, you must keep your individual rhythms. The first beat must be felt."

Soyer added, "The dotted quarter isn't sustained long enough, which makes the eighth note that follows sound like an accent."

Take 6, which Dalley introduced with a loud Bronx cheer, was interrupted when Steinhardt stopped playing and said, "Dave, what happened before J?" Soyer said, "I screwed up. I played all the wrong notes. And, Mike, your solo sounds impassioned—hot, very hot. Could you try it with a little less vibrato?"

They started again. Take 7 was completed without incident, and they went into the control room to listen to it. Tree stayed in the studio and did some stretching exercises for a few minutes, and then came in to listen, too. In the fall, he had said aches and pains were not a problem with him; now he said, "I'm in agony. There isn't one single muscle or bone in my body that isn't throbbing. I'm going to get one of those portable massage tables and have someone come in every day and give me a rubdown." He listened for a few minutes and then mentioned a baseball game he'd seen on television the night before. Tree and Dellheim are both interested in the game—Tree obsessed, actually—and Tree said, "That instant replay sure showed how wrong an umpire can be."

Steinhardt said, "Instant *replay!* My God—think what life would be like for us if there was an instant replay for every mistake we make onstage." Dalley was pretending to strangle himself—hands clutching throat, tongue out, eyes rolling—and Soyer was pacing up and down, smoking.

When the tape ended, Soyer said, "Let's try it one more time." They went out to the studio, tuned again, and played the movement. Dellheim flicked the switch and said, "That's it—I think I've got it."

Soyer asked, "How were the pizzicatos?"

Dellheim's eyebrows cleared the rims of his glasses and he said, "Marvelous! I'm going to take them home in a jar and keep them there. I'll bring them back when I need them." Tree thought Dellheim's "That's it—I think I've got it" the highest praise they received.

The remaining three movements, which they finished by five the following day, were a little less arduous, though the quartet continued to criticize each other, polish fine points.

Tree accused Steinhardt of sliding up to a note. Steinhardt protested, "I have to get there *some* way, and I like the slide —it's not too much."

In the slow movement, Tree said, "It's too Germanic. It sounds like the Martin Bormann Quartet." "The Göring edition," Dalley put in. And Steinhardt summed it up: "It sounds like we're playing for Hitler's wedding." "Also, we're schlepping," Soyer said.

Of a section in the third movement, Tree said, "It sounds like the 'Nutcracker' Suite." Dalley said, "Brahms wouldn't like you to say that. He hated Tchaikovsky," and Tree said, "It was mutual. Tchaikovsky called Brahms's music 'salon music,' and he didn't mean it as a compliment."

Dellheim went into the studio after a take of the last movement (Dalley had facetiously suggested they release the record minus that movement) to talk to them. "It sounds slapdash. You slam into it too much. You need a nice solid forte. And everything sounds so *important* after Bar 276, when it should be hinting at tapering down. And Bar 293—the first note is the end of the phrase, it's true, but you shouldn't drop it like a hot potato."

Dalley suggested that next time perhaps they should record the last movement first, since it is always the most difficult.

Dellheim, eyebrows above glasses, said, "You mean you don't feel a sense of continuity in here?" He went back into the control room, and Begley said, "It's nice to see you earning your money."

After a few more takes, one of which seemed fine to Dellheim, Steinhardt said, "I'd like to do the beginning again —just twelve bars." He played it the way the last take had sounded to him, out of tune, exaggerating to make his point, and Soyer said, "Well, that's a good reason."

Tree said, "I'd like to continue through Bar 24. I have the same pattern you do, Arnold, and I'm not pleased with mine, either." Steinhardt said, "You sounded fine. You're being too fussy," and Tree said, "Nevertheless, I want to do it again. It's Be Kind to Mike Week."

They did the first section and then came into the control room to listen. Tree stretched, sighed, and said, "Brahms had no understanding of recording techniques. Arnold, you get one more chance to play that in tune, and then you've had it. You have to gamble. If this isn't the best, you're going to have to settle for the worst." Tree stopped talking and listened to the take. He said, "It sounds self-pitying." Steinhardt threw back his head and roared. When he'd stopped laughing, he said, "That's the mood I'm in—self-pitying."

Soyer put out his cigarette and said, *"Nu!* Let's give it one more try," and Tree said, "Why is it I grow to *hate* everything we play in here?"

Back in the studio, Steinhardt, striving mightily for perfection, was trying a different fingering. After the first twenty bars, Dellheim flicked the switch and said, "Do you want to hear it?"

They went into the control room to listen, and Steinhardt said, "I'm still not pleased. I want to do it one more time."

Dellheim said, "We *have* a good take—several, in fact."

Steinhardt would have persisted, but Dalley had already left.

(In the spring of 1979, Peter Dellheim was struck down by a ferocious cancer. Throughout a series of painful and debilitating treatments, he continued to go to work. But in the fall of that year, he died. He was always modest about his artistry, and certainly never thought of the hundreds of recordings he was responsible for as a personal tribute, though in view of his contribution to each one, they should be considered as such. The recording sessions continue, supervised by Jack Pfeiffer, though each time they go to RCA the Guarneri expects to find Peter there, and Tree regrets the fact that their last session with Peter—the last of the three Brahms—was such a rough one. "We'd been on tour, and we hadn't rehearsed, and it was grueling for Peter. And though we didn't know, I think Peter knew that he was mortally ill.")

~

In June, the quartet played at Wolf Trap and in Lexington, Kentucky, as they had the year before. They spent three days in New York recording a Mendelssohn and a Beethoven viola quintet with Pinchas Zukerman, who is better known as a violinist but enjoys the variety. Toward the end of the month, Dalley moved his family to their summer home, in Michigan, near Interlochen, and Tree took his to Marlboro, where, for a change, he said, he would be an onlooker rather than a participant. Soyer was looking forward to spending a lot of time on his boat, and Steinhardt planned to take his family to Germany in July, so that his wife could visit her relatives. He would also perform at the Spoleto Festival. Soyer would spend two weeks coaching in Maine, but for the most part all four intended to take it easy during the summer. The 1978–79 season would be an especially demanding one. They would go to Japan at the end of September for two weeks and ten concerts. They would tour Europe in January and Australia in April, and in spite of the fact that their fee had been increased one more time, their American schedule was filling up fast. To their surprise, they were scheduled to spend ten days in Albuquerque for five concerts. A couple of times one or another would call Beall and ask, "Are you *sure* about that?" In February, Soyer, Steinhardt, and Tree had agreed to participate in a fund-raising auction for Stanford University's Lively Arts

Series. They were auctioned off in absentia on May 1, and got letters saying that Steinhardt and Soyer would each give a solo recital and Tree would play tennis.

The final concert of the 1977–78 season was to take place July 2 at the Caramoor Music Festival, in Katonah, New York —where the Guarneri has concluded each season since its inception—but before that the quartet went back to Tampa, on June 26, to give three concerts and two open rehearsals. The pianist Eugene Istomin went, too, to do a Brahms quartet with them, and to hold a master class for the advanced piano students at the University of South Florida. This was the Guarneri's seventh trip to Tampa, and in 1976 the university had awarded the members of the quartet honorary doctoral degrees for "their outstanding contribution to music and their service to this university." John Coker, the university's director of cultural events, has been ingenious in his use of the quartet, and each year something new is tried in an effort to encourage interest in chamber music in Tampa. Coker has had the Guarneri give open rehearsals and coach student quartets, with one man in charge of each session; once, he brought in a fledgling professional quartet, the Columbus Symphony String Quartet—members of the Columbus Symphony—for coaching by the Guarneri.

Coker, a bearded man with a gentle manner, says the Guarneri players bring to teaching "the jovial seriousness that pervades all their activities." Open rehearsals enable students to see how the players work together and also to learn a great deal about music in the process. Coker doesn't think the Guarneri will ever split up. "They know what they themselves can do, and they have professional respect for each other," he says. "They are so secure—individually and as musicians— that they can accept criticism. They don't have any ego problems." Coker always has a meet-the-artists reception after one of the concerts, to break down the invisible barrier that exists between performers and audiences.

The quartet likes Tampa. Over the years, they have made friends there, and in June the climate is right for golf, tennis, sailing. Coker and several other faculty members initiated poker games a few years ago. The Guarneri members—minus Dalley—like to play in a seedy motel, with eyeshades and booze and no women. But the game is serious in its trappings only. The big loser may be out fourteen dollars and change. This year, each gambler was presented with a T-shirt—a picture of the quartet with "We Play Poker Better Than the Guarneri" under it in large letters. Another admirer once had some Guarneri T-shirts printed in New York—a picture of the group over the words "We Play Beethoven." A pupil of Soyer's, wearing one of these shirts, was stopped on Madison Avenue by a woman wearing dark glasses, who scrutinized his chest for some time. Then, breaking into a broad smile, she said, "And very well, too!"

PART IV

Ask the quartet about a foreign tour: theirs is apt to be a gourmand's memory. The small town where they had wild boar looms larger than Berlin, at least for a moment. The comforts and pleasures of seventeen concerts in twenty days are few. A decent hotel. Crossing paths with fellow-musician friends. Weather that does not result in canceled flights. Luggage that arrives on the same plane as they. The absence of bureaucratic red tape. The audiences in Europe are good— wonderful, actually. It's a rare audience that doesn't ask for and get several encores. (Yehudi Menuhin once said that after a concert in America, people come backstage to congratulate him. In Europe, they ask how he fingered a certain passage.) Rarely do they get to take their families along, and it is their most extended period away from home.

Some of their experiences in Europe have been harrowing. They played in Spain in 1977, and in Bilbao—a hotbed of political dissension, and the seat of the Separatist Basque movement—after the concert, no one came backstage. Tree says, "We packed up our instruments and left the hall. The street was dark and deserted, and we were easily a mile from our hotel. The good people who had come to the concert had taken the last of the taxis. We didn't know where the hell we were, or how to get back to the hotel." There had been daily reports in the newspapers of violence in the streets, assassinations. For many of their concerts—not licensed by the government and hence not taxable to the sponsors in Spain—they were paid in pesetas. The catch was that they couldn't take the money out of the country. This night, they started to walk, randomly. Tree remembers coming on an enormous building that took up an entire city block. Soyer spotted a soldier in a sentry box; they went up to him to ask directions, and, Soyer says, "We were immediately surrounded by soldiers, rifles drawn." Tree says, "We must have been a suspicious bunch —Dave, with his cello, looking ominous; Arnold, a foot taller than anyone they'd ever seen in their lives; and me. I was wearing a green beret, the symbol of the Separatist movement. None of us spoke much Spanish—mine sounds like German. Finally, I reached in my pocket for a postcard with a picture of our hotel." Tree thinks they looked so inept and rattled (possibly it was Tree's blush) that the soldiers believed they were musicians and not murderers, and pointed them toward their hotel.

In Madrid, the night before they were to leave for Portugal, they got a call from the cellist Paul Tortellier, who was staying in the same hotel and planned to leave for Paris in the morning. He told them he was very worried about the situation, and that they should be, too. He said that the soprano Elizabeth Schwarzkopf had been detained at the airport and held overnight for trying to take currency out of the country. As it happened, the Guarneri had bundles of it. They talked to their manager, who suggested they put it in their shoes. There was so much, Steinhardt says, "That would have made me four inches taller." They decided to risk it—go to the airport and see what happened. They carried the money in their pockets—wads of it. "Like an enormous growth," Tree says. Each man was searched by a guard (Tree had a flash fantasy of never seeing his family again) and allowed to leave the country. Perhaps it was their openness: they made no attempt to conceal the money. Perhaps the guards were actually looking for weapons. They're in no hurry to go back.

In Australia, a year later, they were paid in cash for a seven-city tour, at the last stop, Sydney. Nothing illegal, just the custom, and the money could be taken out of the country. It was delivered in a suitcase to their hotel, to Steinhardt's room. Tree says, "We dumped it on the bed, a *pile* of money —almost to the ceiling. Arnold called room service, and when the waiter came in he looked surprised at the sight of us—four Americans, with our jackets off, splitting all this money four ways. Arnold glared at him and said, 'You haven't seen a thing.' "

~

In the fall of 1979, the quartet went to Japan for the first time. Soyer, who is in charge of overseas arrangements, urged the others to leave for Tokyo early enough to give them at least a day to recover from the vast time difference and especially severe cases of jet lag. Dalley chose to leave later than the others, and he arrived in Tokyo on the day of the first concert. They played twice in Tokyo and in six other cities, including Osaka, Fukuoka, Fujisawa, and Kagoshima. They were provided with an interpreter, who took charge of everything—baggage, reservations, tickets—and they were surprised at how dependent they were on him. The only time the four don't shoot off in as many different directions is when they are giving a concert, and sometimes when they are rehearsing, and none of them envies the interpreter's task in looking after them while they were there. Tree says, "We can be so abstracted, impractical, thoughtless. We would never have survived without him." With the exception of RCA executives working in the country, they met very few people who spoke English. Soyer says, "When we strayed off the beaten path, away from tourist attractions and without our interpreter, we got hopelessly lost. We carried printed cards with the names of our hotels at all times—just in case."

Soyer describes the audiences as being moderate in every respect—in size and in response—and always pleasant. Steinhardt says, "They were attentive and polite, and so eerily *silent* that sometimes I would look out between movements to make sure there *was* an audience." Beall is grateful that the quartet has a manager in Germany who handles foreign tours. And in each city they go to, there is a local representative, which the men refer to as a manager—for lack of a different word, such as "auspices." Dalley feels that the manager for the Japanese tour was not the best, and that their tour wasn't sufficiently publicized, though Tree says, "We had lots of press conferences—run with the formality of a General Assembly session —and because of the publicity, as the tour progressed our audiences increased."

One of the bonuses of their grueling life, in addition to the music they play, is usually the post-concert talk with audience members who come backstage. (In many places there would be more if the four musicians weren't somewhat awesome onstage.) Some fans they've met after concerts in distant cities have become lifelong friends. The men are, by nature, gregarious, and the steam built up in the course of a concert— euphoria, when all goes well—can be let off somewhat by talking to people who have heard them play. Of the Japanese experience, Soyer says, "The interpreter was helpful, but we all felt frustrated by the secondhand communication." Steinhardt observes, "The differences in culture and religion are tremendous. You shouldn't be fooled by the fact that the men wear business suits and make motorcycles and pianos, and all those things one thinks of as Western. They're interested in all those things, yet they're *not* Western. While you're in Japan, it seems like a contradiction." Soyer adds, "The Japanese aren't well acquainted with chamber music yet. They primarily like orchestras and soloists—violinists and pianists." One Japanese pianist, a Juilliard graduate, estimates that eighty percent of the homes in Japan have a piano in the living room, and someone studying the instrument. Dalley says, "I was amazed to see on television, on prime time, a violin teacher giving a lesson to a class of a dozen or so pupils. Of course, Suzuki"—who starts his pupils with a rote approach, pupils mimicking the teacher and not learning to read notes until the technique is fairly secure—"claims that just as anyone can learn to drive a car, anyone can learn to play the violin." The idea makes Dalley blanch.

Soyer has a friend in Tokyo, a Japanese cellist who was off teaching in Kyoto when the quartet was in Tokyo. Soyer says, "He sent his wife to the concert, and she brought her niece, to act as interpreter. She came with gifts. They are all great gift-givers. They *shower* you with gifts."

The quartet members were rather stunned at how crowded the country is—how many people live on that little island. Steinhardt says, "One city melts into another. The homes are necessarily small, and we were told that most entertaining is done in restaurants, at night." Tree says, "In the time Dave and I spent having lunch in a sushi bar"—by the end of the tour they were almost addicted to raw fish—"two or three tablefuls next to us had come and gone. They just don't sit for an hour at lunch."

Steinhardt regrets the fact that they had so little time in Japan. "We missed the shrines and the beautiful mountain areas, but at least we saw Kagoshima. It's on a bay, and the countryside is stunning. And there is a volcano that was actually coughing up—spitting up—lava. We saw a woman in a beautiful dress—white silk, with obi in the back. It was a sunny, perfect day, and she was carrying an umbrella. At first it looked like a joke—a gag. We couldn't figure it out. And then we realized that soot is constantly filtering down from the volcano—hour after hour after hour."

Tree took his tennis racket along, and several games were arranged for him. He says, "The Japanese excel at *everything,* and the competition was stiff. Because of the tremendous numbers of people and the size of the country, they've changed the rules of the game. The etiquette is different. It's considered bad form for two people to take up a court, and if a game is tied, five–five, the first side to get a point wins the match."

Tree stayed behind to record the two Mozart duos for violin and viola with his old colleague from Curtis, Toshiya Eto. Eto, who was under Hurok management and had a successful career in America in the sixties, is Japan's most renowned violinist—a national hero. Tree and Eto spent several days in a mountain village, Niko. RCA moved recording equipment into the town hall there. Tree says, "Every single Japanese wears a wristwatch you've never seen the likes of in America. Black-and-white television is unknown there. And their recordings are of the best quality imaginable. The equipment is sophisticated, and the standards *so* high. I've never worked so hard as I did recording those two duos with Toshiya. I was ready for a hospital bed." Tree never listens to records he has had any part of—he calls it a superstition. But the Mozart record—which is selling like hot cakes in Japan but has not been released here, and which he has given to friends —attests to the fact that in describing the high quality of Japanese recording, Tree, who has a tendency to exaggerate, is speaking literally.

On January 10, 1980, the quartet left Kennedy Airport at midnight, in a raging rainstorm, for their fifteenth European tour: London, Rotterdam, Brussels, Paris, Budapest (for the first time), Mannheim, Detmold, Hamburg, Cologne, Iserlohn, Hanover, Düsseldorf, and Lausanne. Janet Soyer was tempted to go along, to see Budapest, but the men would be there for only a day and a half, and the day would be Sunday, when everything, they'd been told, would be closed. It was an especially hectic schedule, and no one was looking forward to it. Steinhardt says, "It was unrelenting. It was too long—I was reeling." But he adds, "The worse it gets, the more we take pleasure and sustenance in the music—the concerts themselves."

They always enjoy going to London. Over the years, they've made many friends there, and they like the audiences. Steinhardt says, "The English don't overwhelm you with the sheer volume of their applause. It's quiet. You think, 'Oh, my gosh, we didn't do very well.' But then the applause continues in that fashion for a long time. There'll be a few bravos, of course, but it's not the kind of thundering ovation we get in, say, Germany."

There were slowdowns at the London airport, and they got to Rotterdam in the nick of time for their concert there. The connection to Brussels was smooth, but the hotel was a dump, and they moved. In Paris, just before they went out to play, according to Steinhardt, their manager said, " 'Play pretty. The concert is being broadcast throughout Europe. Fifty-two million people will be listening.' No psychologist she."

They were looking forward to a full day in Paris, just

larking around. Instead, they discovered they didn't have the proper papers for entry into Budapest, their next stop. (Dalley had planned to go to Stuttgart on his free day, to see his friend Walter Hamma, a violin dealer, "the last of a breed," who not only sells violins but makes them, too. Dalley says, "He'll retire soon, and he has no apprentice to replace him." Soyer tells the story: "We went to the Hungarian embassy, on the same square where Rubinstein lives—a beautiful little cul-de-sac—only to be told we were in the wrong building, that we had to go way the hell to the opposite end of Paris, the other side of the Seine, to the consulate, in Montparnasse. Also, we needed two additional passport photographs. We got a cab and told the driver what the situation was. Parisian cabdrivers have a terrible reputation for being nasty—especially to foreigners—but this guy was fantastic. He found a photograph place on the street and he *waited* for us while we had our pictures taken, and then he took us to the Hungarian consulate." (When they got back home, friends asked, "How was Paris?" "Lunch cost forty-five dollars.")

They found the Budapest airport to be gloomy, shabby, and grim. "Lots of red tape and waiting," Soyer says. "They're very suspicious. They check you against your photograph two or three times in several different places." Dalley says, "The outskirts of Budapest were ugly, but the inner city, with the Danube flowing through, was nice." They stayed at the Budapest Hilton, and again their concert was broadcast. They were paid in forints, which they couldn't take out of the country. They couldn't pay their hotel bill with them, either, because the Budapest Hilton would not accept them. Tree says of the money, "There wasn't anything to buy in Budapest that we couldn't get in New York—cheaper. We might as well have handed it out on the street, and said, 'Here, go buy yourself a banana split.' "

But the audience was one of the most enthusiastic they'd ever had. Steinhardt says, "They clap in unison, in a rhythm that slowly begins to gather speed. It's like a choo-choo train. If they're asking for an encore, it's almost menacing. 'You better play—or else.' " They played four. There were three quartets in the audience, including the Bartók, a formidable group, well known in America through concerts and records. The Guarneri had met the group in New York, when the Bartók played with the Chamber Music Society. And several years earlier, Soyer had very nearly sold his Guarneri to the Hungarian government, which provides the quartet with its instruments. Many musicians are ambivalent about their instruments at times. Old ones, especially, react to changes in temperature and humidity. Soyer was considering buying a Goffriller, so his cello was shipped to Budapest, to be tried by the cellist in the Bartók. He's pleased that his cello was turned down, in favor of Martin Lovett's Montagnana. The cellist himself was squeezed out of the quartet, for what Soyer calls "some political hanky-panky. He was summarily fired. He was at the concert, alone." After the concert, they went to a café and heard some authentic gypsy fiddling. It made the whole trip worthwhile.

Steinhardt says, "In Europe, for me, the high point in terms of how we are received—and this has been true for nine years in a row—is Detmold, where Brahms once lived. The conservatory there is one of the most well known in Europe. The audience is a combination of faculty members, students, and townspeople. We always have to play three or four encores. They won't let us off the stage."

In Hamburg, the Brahms Quartet was in the audience, and after the concert, the cellist came backstage and handed Soyer a picture of himself and Janet, wearing cowboy hats, taken in Albuquerque the previous spring. Soyer says, "We were walking around the Old Market section, and this young man was following us around, ducking behind trees, taking pictures. I finally stopped and confronted him. 'Why are you taking pictures?' He said, 'You're Mr. Soyer. I'm the cellist in the Brahms Quartet, and I wanted a picture of you in your cowboy hat.' "

Their friend Pinchas Zukerman was in Hamburg with Marc Neikrug—the two were giving a concert there the next night—and after the performance they all went out to dinner.

The rest of the tour went like clockwork—the kind of European travel they like: good trains, short distances, fine food, no passport hassles. Friends along the way, and the end in sight.

~

The quartet returned from Europe on February 1st, and on the fourth, with bad cases of jet lag—each man kept waking at four in the morning—they began rehearsing for concerts scheduled for February 6, 7, 8, 9, and 10, in four different halls in New York and with four completely different programs. As Dalley points out, after the strenuous European tour, when they get home it is not unusual for someone to get sick. This year, it was Soyer. He had a virus—aching bones and a fever. The first two concerts would be a "Guarneri & Friends" at Alice Tully Hall, with the pianist Misha Dichter, and Jaime Laredo playing viola.

On Monday, the fourth, they met in Soyer's apartment to discuss business. Usually, business with Beall is attended to on days when the quartet is in New Jersey, rehearsing at Dalley's house. Beall lives nearby. He says the only time he sees them in the city is when one or another is having a bow rehaired, and pops into his office to say hello. Once Beall went out to La Guardia Airport in hopes of talking to the four, but Dalley had gone through security and was not at the designated meeting place. A visit from Beall is apt to result in his being a target for, if not rosin cakes, epithets. It's hard for him to get an answer out of them—hard for him to get all of them to even listen to the question—and since all decisions must be agreed upon, Beall can't make any progress until he does. While Beall is there, Steinhardt is apt to continue to practice, and say, "Give my share to charity. I do this for love, not money." If someone calls Beall and asks him if the quartet is in town, chances are he'll say, "No, thank God."

After the meeting—unknowingly, they had again agreed to one hundred sixteen concerts, twenty-four more than their self-imposed limit—Soyer called Steinhardt and told him to come to Dichter's—that they would be doing the A Major, which Steinhardt plays. The programs, already printed, listed the Brahms G Minor Quartet, which Dalley plays, and which he'd come prepared to rehearse, but Dichter reported that Lockwood had told him he was to do the Brahms A Major, which Philippe Entremont thought he would be playing with the quartet in March. Although when the quartet formed, Sasha Schneider said Dalley should play violin in piano quartets, which require only one violin, Dalley, by choice, plays first infrequently these days. He doesn't like the extra rehearsing, and his ego apparently doesn't require massaging, as Sasha's did.

On Tuesday afternoon, the four rehearsed again, this time in Alice Tully Hall. They had the use of the stage starting at one. Although the quartet doesn't care where they rehearse, it's essential for a pianist to get a workout on the piano he'll be using at the concert. Soyer, whose temperature had reached 102, was wearing a fisherman's thick knit sweater over a flannel shirt, and blue jeans. He looked pale, almost gray, and he didn't say "So . . . *Nu?*" once. Dichter, a handsome, boyish-looking man of medium height, with powerful shoulder and arm muscles that attest to a lifetime of piano practicing and playing, was wearing a striped T-shirt and corduroy jeans. Steinhardt had on a plaid flannel shirt and denim pants, and Tree a crisp checked shirt and tan slacks.

Sometimes, as today, when they are tired and pressed for time, someone watching them settle into a rehearsal might have a feeling of being buzzed by mosquitoes. The three strings played the introductory phrase of the Brahms in unison —Cobbett describes it as having "Olympian serenity"—in preparation for the piano's entrance. A few minutes into the piece, in a passage for strings only, they stopped. Tree said, "In the beginning, we used to start with an up bow," and he added, "It's too *loud."* "The crescendo is a little overpowering," Steinhardt said, and then, "Isn't that nicer? To come down a little?" Soyer said, "It's not balanced," and Steinhardt said, "It sounds like you're accenting the first note, Dave." Soyer sang the phrase. "You mean that?" He played it again. "Now you're accenting *all* the notes," Steinhardt said. Soyer looked annoyed. "How else am I going to play it? You're two octaves higher, and it's much louder than what I'm doing, Arnold." Steinhardt said, "Well, it sounds to me as if you're making a big accent at the beginning of that phrase." "Well, I'm not." Tree said, "It's not a question of attack or accent. Before, you were getting a little more into the string, Dave. Do you want me to do what you're doing, too?" Soyer said, "I don't *consider* that an accent." Steinhardt imitated how it had sounded to him. "But I'm not *doing* that, Arnold. I'm just starting a note." Steinhardt said, "You're making an accent." Soyer said, "I don't know what you *mean,* making an accent. Do you mean a forzando?" Steinhardt nodded. "On the F-sharp . . . But that's not what I've been doing." Tree said, "Dave, Arnold is a little more sustained," and Soyer said impatiently, "But I have no *choice*. I have to get to the A—a big leap." ("You did." "I did not." "You did *too*." "I *did not!*") They seemed to be talking at once, solving nothing, but finally they played the phrase with no interruptions, and Dichter, who had been waiting for his cue, joined in.

Tree and Steinhardt played with legs crossed or feet tapping. Soyer smoked while he played, the cigarette held between the third and fourth fingers of his bow hand. Dichter smoked a cigar, and each time he lit it, showing a rather zany respect for the stage floor, he put the matchstick on the Steinway concert grand. The casual dress and the bantering—the four are long-time friends—was in startling contrast to the regal, royal hall, its plush purple seats ringing back and upward, a splendid reminder of the concert that would follow, the next night. Musicians walk down three steep flights from the street to get to the Tully Hall stage area—not an unusual concert-hall arrangement—and during a pause Dichter asked Tree, "Does it make you nervous, being this far down?"

Tree said, "I do my best playing underground."

"In Holland," Dichter said, "after a flood, we're the first to go."

Steinhardt asked Soyer how he felt. Soyer said, "Lousy. I'll feel worse tomorrow, and by Thursday I'll be hopeless."

Dichter asked Soyer, "Is it all right with your doctor—that you haven't canceled?" and Soyer said, "Yes, he wants to hear the concert." (Actually, if they had not, in effect, tied up two guest artists—kept them from playing other concerts—they might have canceled. Besides wives, only people like George Mittag and Chester Chorny, who are in charge of the backstage area at Grace Rainey Rogers, know how often a musician who should really be home in bed performs anyway, with no bad effect on the performance. Mittag and Chorny are fiercely protective of the artists—Chorny straightens Soyer's tie as a matter of course, and brushes his jacket, too, before the four go onstage. Chorny, years after the event, still regrets the time he failed to provide warm water for Isaac Stern, so Stern could warm his hands before he went out to play, though he was touched when Stern said, "I learned a new trick. I play better with cold hands." Also, he doesn't like to think about the night Peter Serkin, with a terrible cold, played the Beethoven "Diabelli" Variations—fifty-three minutes—and held in a racking cough until he was offstage.)

Someone else would have the use of the hall at four, so they worked with unusual intensity, trying to beat the clock. They stopped often to dissect a phrase. Of one, Steinhardt said, "*Spread* it a bit—it's so *tight.*" They repeated it, his way, and Dichter said, "That was nice. What's the tab?" Steinhardt said, arms flung out, grinning, with a Yiddish shrug, "So good, and it's the same price. You get jello, bread and butter, coffee . . ."

Cobbett also says of the A Major that "Brahms had no scruples in writing orchestrally for the piano, and the pianist who incautiously lets himself go will find himself playing wrong notes, and, if asked to correct these, he will complain that the passage is badly written for accurate playing with full tone. This is true."

Now Dichter stopped and said he wanted to go over a development section. "It starts at letter I. Is four measures before enough?" Steinhardt said, "It certainly is. We're professionals." Dichter practiced the passage. Then he played it with both hands—notes written for one—and said, "That's my problem." Soyer said, "I didn't know you only had one hand, Misha." Dichter has a marvelous strong, firm, and, when necessary, light touch—not a pianist who would bury string players with the rich Brahms piano part. They were using different editions, and he periodically got up to compare parts with Steinhardt or Soyer or Tree. He looked startled at a subito piano and then a pause that wasn't in his score, and Steinhardt said, "That's one of our patented ideas. The audience gets to fill in notes in the pause." Music can be their source of energy, and as they rehearsed they grew more animated; even Soyer perked up. Tree positively lit up—blue eyes darting to Soyer, to Steinhardt; frequently he grinned with pleasure. Soyer said during a pause, "This is how it sounded in Germany in Brahms's time." He played a heavy, solid, plodding legato, with thick, syrupy slurs. Steinhardt said, "Let's all have a little bit of that—move this over to Eighty-sixth and York, and play a little out of tune too."

Soyer said to Dichter, "Don't you want to stretch that phrase out a bit?" and Dichter said, "Yes, I thought of that after I played it. This is not Brahms's best section." Tree added, "This is where his seams are showing. On the record, we did it this way": he played a phrase emphasizing a rhythmic pattern. "The way we're doing it now, it sounds as if we're tumbling."

After a particularly dense piano passage that worked, Dichter said, "It was just luck that I managed that," and Tree laughed and said, "You're an honest person, Misha." They played on, and Steinhardt said, "We're not dovetailing."

Charles Wadsworth walked down the aisle and called out, "How's the piano, Misha?"

Dichter just shrugged, and Tree said, "A piano is a piano." Bill Lockwood joined Wadsworth, and said, "I just talked to Entremont, in Paris. He doesn't play the G Minor. He'd rather do the Fauré. He does *not* send you his regards, Misha." Dichter looked surprised, and then distinctly annoyed. He plays all three Brahms quartets—in fact, he had done them in one evening at Jaime Laredo's Y series. (A mistake, all agreed. Too much.) But the works are formidable for the piano, and in addition to this program, he was giving a solo recital (all Liszt) in Tully Hall the following Sunday. Lockwood said jovially, "It's not *my* mistake. I know the difference between major and minor—minor is lower case." Tree smiled at the joke, but Dichter just shrugged.

Lockwood and Wadsworth left, and the four continued. Tree said, "That phrase should be broader—potbellied," and to Steinhardt and Soyer, "I wouldn't take it poisonal, but you two are doing exactly what you pounced on *me* for doing the first time we played that theme."

Soyer said, "It's unrelentingly loud, and that's not all that's wrong with it." He played a phrase and sang it at the same time. "It's a terrible bowing. It sounds like jellyfish."

Dichter abruptly segued into a Brahms concerto, and Steinhardt a Schubert Fantasy—a fleet, fast, showcase solo. Dichter switched gears and accompanied Steinhardt. Soyer noodled at the "Meditation" from *Thais* and asked, "Does anyone have Mischa Elman's recording of this?"

Back to Brahms: Tree said to Steinhardt, "We're together there, and you're doing something ad lib with your part. Let me *know* what you're going to do. This is the most damned difficult piece in the *world.*" Steinhardt's "ad lib" was in the upper stratosphere, but Dichter stopped and said, "Arnold, that's *octavo* in my score"—an octave higher. Steinhardt threw his head back and laughed; played it higher, with exaggerated squeaks; and returned to the correct position.

Soyer said, "I'm voicing my opinion now, in case anyone wants to change it, but it sounds tentative and *amateurish.* And it should be very *massive* in here." They continued, and Tree said, "I have all these chromaticisms, but no one listens."

The slow movement is plaintive, poignant, with an almost swaying rhythm, and Soyer exaggerated it and said, "Offenbach wrote this; it's called the 'Barcarole.' It sounds very loud before K. Is it all that important?" He added, to Dichter, "It sounds like we're swamped."

Dichter said he'd be careful, and Soyer said, "I don't want you to be careful. I think we should work something out."

In the third movement, Tree said, "This is the most ungain - ly thing in the repertoire." Dichter said, "It sounds agitated," and Steinhardt said, "It's an accurate reflection of how I feel. My heart is going double time."

By four o'clock, they had made their way through the piece, with perhaps a hundred interruptions to discuss fine points. Dichter's cigar had become a soggy stogy, and, chomping on it, he played a Scott Joplin rag. He stopped, and said he'd like to play the quartet through, without interruption. Their demeanor changed; it was, mentally and musically, concert time. They were well into the Adagio when a stagehand opened the great slatted door and told them they would have to stop. The artist scheduled to perform that night had the use of the hall from four to six. The men continued to play and then reluctantly stopped. While Soyer, Steinhardt, and Tree were packing up their instruments, Dichter said, "Let's go out for pizza." Tree begged off; he had to go have some music photocopied. Soyer was going home and to bed. Steinhardt said, "O.K., Misha, as long as it's good and hot and quick. I have to meet someone downtown at five." Dichter swept the matchsticks off the piano into his palm and dumped them in an ashtray offstage. Soyer asked the stage manager who was performing later that week. He was told Carlos Tolen-tino. Soyer said, "There was a famous bullfighter with that name. . . ."

~

On Wednesday, the quartet had a marathon rehearsal in the Steinhardts' apartment on Riverside Drive. Starting at one, they rehearsed the Mozart "Dissonant" Quartet; the Beethoven C Major Quartet, Opus 59, No. 3; the Mozart Viola Quintet in D Major; and the Dvořák Terzetto for Two Violins and Viola, Opus 74, for which Dalley and Tree would play violin and Steinhardt viola. (With the exception of the Mozart quintet, this would be their Friday-night Grace Rainey Rogers program, which Tree had picked. Hilde Limondjian had called him just before the quartet left for Europe, and said she needed to know what the program would be, to get it to the printer on time. Tree couldn't reach the others, so, on the spur of the moment, he made the choices himself. Too late, he realized each of the pieces was in the key of C major. He confided later, "We're a very argumentative group. If anyone does anything the others object to, he is sure to be *pounced* on. I'll be curious to see how soon they notice what I've done. There's practically a mystique about programming—having pieces in different keys, the relationship of one key to another. Personally, I think it's a lot of nonsense.")

The Steinhardts' living room, which overlooks the Drive, and provides a good view of the Hudson River and New Jersey, was crowded with a grand piano, several armchairs, and two sofas, all pushed against the walls to make room for the stands and chairs. Soyer felt worse than he had the day before. The fever, his inactivity—all that time in bed —had left him weak and wobbly. He showed them a cable he'd received from their European manager. They were being asked to play an additional concert on their 1981 European tour, bringing the total to eighteen concerts in twenty days. The message seemed more a demand than a request. Soyer says, "Managers are often inhumane. Not out of malice. They just don't think. As far as they're concerned, we're robots. Wind us up, and we'll play. They don't stop to think of what's involved for *us*. Schlepping around with a lot of baggage, being exhausted . . . ."

They had all unpacked their instruments and were ready to begin. Soyer threw the cable on the floor, and they started. As usual, they got hung up on the opening—a twenty-two-bar adagio introduction, with such sword-piercing dissonances (hence the name "Dissonant") that some musicians in Mozart's time succumbed to the temptation to correct them. The music is pessimistic, melancholy, and stunning in its beauty. They played the introduction, and Tree said to Steinhardt, "The last three bars, before the allegro, take time on the basis of what we do. *Listen* to us." Steinhardt said, "I always listen when you play." Tree said they were distorting wildly, and Steinhardt quipped, "You never complained before." Tree said, "Well, I'm complaining now. Let's go back to the top." They started and then stopped when Tree said to Dalley, "No vibrato?" Dalley said, "Not until the motion starts." Tree looked surprised, but nodded agreement. Soyer, whose part was tempo-setting, quiet eighth notes, was not involved in the vibrato discussion. They began again and stopped again. Tree said, "You know, Arnold, we used to play it all in one bow," and Steinhardt said, "I find it cramped now." They decided not to rehearse the slow movement, and skipped the repeats in the Minuetto—something they would not do at the concert, and something an amateur would do only if his clothes were on fire.

Soyer has said, "John and I agree that the Mozart quartets, with the exception of one or two, don't wear as well for us as the Haydn." (A constant reminder of Tree's throughout a season is "Boys, you've got to decide which Haydn we're going to do next season.") "We can play a Haydn seventy times, and always find something fresh. And we feel the same way about the Beethovens. It's purely subjective. The other two guys don't feel that way. Arnold and Michael will get tired of Beethoven more readily than they do of Mozart. Interestingly enough, that was the case with the Budapest Quartet. They had the same split feelings about those things. For Joe Roisman and Mischa, the Beethoven quartets were always new and fresh. With Boris and Sasha, it was the Mozart."

Perhaps in deference to Soyer and Dalley, more probably because the Mozart is far less demanding than the Beethoven, they spent a minimum amount of time on the Mozart. The Beethoven, the last of three commissioned by Count Rasumovsky and named for him, is included in the middle period, but many musicians feel that perhaps the three are the most difficult instrumentally and even musically of all his quartets. A stranger listening to the Guarneri rehearse No. 3 that day might feel that they barely knew the work—that they were just learning it. There were countless arguments about big points and little details—for example, a five-minute argument about where a stringendo began: five, six, or seven bars from the end. There were discrepancies in the markings each had in his score, and at one point, Tree said, "Just once, in fifteen years, we ought to be together." Soyer says of such nattering, "Actually, that's true of everything we play, and I wouldn't have it any other way. We don't stay the same. We change as musicians, and we change as people. It would be dreadful if we played every piece the same way we did ten years ago. If we recorded the Beethoven quartets again, they'd be *very* different. After all, we recorded them years ago. We don't play them the same way. Not that it's better or worse. Just different. Different things are important to us. Perhaps it's maturity, development. Over the years, you can find new things in any work. It's fascinating."

At one point, Steinhardt's son, Alexander (whose birth was announced to a Y audience by Steinhardt blowing a kiss), appeared in the doorway. Soyer, perking up, said, "Sasha, come here!" Steinhardt said, "He doesn't answer to that anymore. He wasn't named for Sasha. On the other hand, he wasn't *not* named for him."

Dalley said, "The more I think about that cable, the madder it makes me. If they want to sabotage the whole tour, this is the way to do it."

The last movement of the Beethoven, a Molto Allegro, ends with a fugue, which the viola begins. Hence, Tree sets the tempo. Soyer likes to tell about the time they played it in Eindhoven, Holland. "Mike said just before we went out to play, 'I think I'll try that fugue a little slower.' Well, it was *slow,* and we were so unaccustomed to the tempo that we were just floundering. It felt like a whole other piece. When it was over, we practically yanked Michael off the stage. *Everybody* boxed his ears—figuratively. 'What the *hell* do you think you're doing?' And so on. We played that movement as an encore, and Michael was so shook up by all the threats of bodily harm that he started it twice as fast as we'd ever played it, which made it doubly difficult. It went like the *wind."*

Today, too, it seemed to be going like the wind, yet Soyer said, "That tempo seems slow to me." Now *he* was pounced on. Dalley said, "Are you crazy?" And Steinhardt said, "What has Janet been feeding you? Are you taking fast pills?"

They were noodling at different spots, practicing, arguing, when Jaime Laredo arrived, directly from the airport. The men were so preoccupied, they didn't stop to say hello. Laredo, a handsome, dark-haired man, was in his travel clothes: a gray suit, complete with vest, and a striped tie. (Laredo came to Curtis from Bolivia when he was thirteen.

Tree, Dalley, and Steinhardt were already at Curtis, and they remember the plump, jolly little boy with the phenomenal talent. Dalley even remembers Laredo's first recital there, and what he played—effortlessly.) Laredo said affably, "What have I done to deserve this warm welcome?" Soyer stopped to say hello, and moved his stand and chair over to make room for him. Laredo unpacked his viola and sat down. It's an Amati —rare and priceless—and Soyer admired it. Tree said, while Laredo tuned, "It sounds effeminate to me." Laredo laughed and said, "You'll be sorry you said that. I'll get you tonight."

Dorothea Steinhardt, who had made coffee and set out, on the dining-room table, bagels, various cheeses, carrot cake, and pastries, appeared in the doorway and asked if they wanted to take a break. Steinhardt said, "We don't have time. Maybe you could bring it in here." She looked at the cluttered room, shrugged, and retreated.

If Soyer sometimes tires of a Mozart quartet, he has no complaints about the viola quintets, and the D Major is a beauty. The slow movement, too, is filled with dissonances, and they give the listener a feeling of being, in slow motion, lofted into the air, suspended, and suddenly dropped, only to be lofted up again. Laredo asked if they were going to take the repeats, and before they answered he reminded them that the Brahms piano quartet lasted fifty minutes. Tree looked incredulous, and said, "Really?" Soyer said he thought that they should take the repeats, nevertheless, and Laredo smiled and said, "There's someone with conviction—character." In the middle of the first movement, Tree asked Laredo if he was comfortable with the tempo. Laredo said he was, and why did Tree ask. "You're our guest," Tree said, "and we want you to be comfortable." He added, to Steinhardt, "I've been here so long I feel I've moved in—that I should be paying rent."

At one point, Soyer reminded Tree that he, Tree, was

supposed to be leading. Tree said, "I feel very threatened by all of you. I thought I *was* leading. I'll make it stronger." Dalley said, "It's dangerously not together," and Steinhardt said, "It shouldn't end with a *whonk!* And don't jump on the downbeat. It sounds like I was banged on the head." Laredo said, "It sounds so flabby," and Tree asked, "Would you say that's a fair appraisal of how we feel?" And at one point he said to Soyer, who now looked flushed and feverish, *"Dave! I don't know this piece well enough for that. Come in when you're supposed to, please!"* Steinhardt said, "He wants to make sure we all play well enough before he comes in." Laredo said, "Arnold, that sounds a little too free," and Steinhardt said, "I wasn't trying to be free. I was just out of control." The dissonances in the slow movement have a gravitational pull, and Tree said, "Arnold, you're playing *with* me. You're supposed to be against me." Steinhardt grinned and asked, "How do we sound together?"

Occasionally, they compared scores with Laredo's, which was leatherbound and a different edition. They teased him about his score, and his Accutron watch, which Dalley said would stop giving the correct time when the government changed in Bolivia. Tree and Laredo were having fun playing the two viola parts, and at times they grinned at each other, and swayed, as if—at least from the waist up—they were waltzing. Laredo sometimes took exception to what the others were doing. "I *hate* that ritard at the end." Tree said, "I may have done it too much, just to test the wind. This is *hard work.*" Steinhardt said, "It's so fancy. Why shouldn't it just be straight ahead?"

At six, they called it quits, and Tree, Dalley, and Steinhardt agreed to meet at Tully Hall the following evening at six-thirty, before the second "Guarneri & Friends" concert, to rehearse the Dvořák.

~

When the quartet formed, Rudolf Serkin urged them to make a point of playing with other musicians. An exchange of musical ideas is healthy, he told them. It would help them avoid the pitfalls of becoming set in their ways, rigid, and it would broaden them to be exposed to other musical ideas. Serkin himself started the trend of concert artists making music together in a series at Grace Rainey Rogers, for which, in 1958, Tree was one of the guest artists. While all the quartet's New York concerts are fully subscribed, and all have long waiting lists in case there are any dropouts among the subscribers, their "Guarneri & Friends" series are perhaps the most popular. The list of their guest artists suggests a *Who's Who* in music, and includes, in part: Murray Perahia, Claude Frank, Julius Levine, Eugene Istomin, Harold Wright, Barry Tuckwell, Jorge Bolet, Walter Trampler, Bernard Greenhouse, Leonard Rose, Anton Kuerti, Garrick Ohlsson, Jean-Bernard Pommier, Jean-Pierre Rampal, Pinchas Zukerman, Emanuel Ax, Oscar Shumsky, Rudolf Firkusny, Lee Luvisi, and, in her first chamber-music performance in America, Alicia de Larrocha. Musicians love to play with the quartet. Misha Dichter, a man of few words, says, "It's fun." And Barry Tuckwell, acknowledged to be the greatest horn player in the world, who has played with all the major quartets, says the difference between the Guarneri and the others is "as cheese is to chalk." Perhaps, since the musicians are having so much fun onstage, the audience has more fun, too.

And even with "company," the quartet never *looks* like a quartet. Alexander Schneider, when he's had some schnapps and has an audience, imitates each man as he walks onstage. They come out in the order in which they will be seated, of course—Tree, Soyer, Dalley, Steinhardt. They don't appear, as some quartets do, to be psychologically joined at the hip, or, as others do, to consist of a slightly bullying leader with three followers. They look like four soloists who, by accident, are on the same stage at the same time. Yet they also look pleased to be with one another. The music they carry onstage is tattered and torn. Much of Steinhardt's is cut. When he has a difficult page turn, he simply slices the page in half. He calls these his Dutch doors. Steinhardt uses a long black velvet padded cloth, which he slings over his shoulder to lessen the gap between violin and collarbone. Sometimes he smacks the rosin dust out of it before he starts to play.

As the four are settling down onstage, one might make a comment to another that will provoke a grin. After the first movement, while the ushers let latecomers in, Steinhardt scans the audience, as if he's looking for a friend or, possibly, counting the house. They are probably the only quartet in the world who have attracted Beatles-type fans. One, in Tampa, invariably tries to engage a seatmate in a discussion of which one, acknowledging applause, *bows* the best. Soyer gets extra points for his, though it's not too deep, because he's carrying the cello. Steinhardt folds at the waist—the deepest bow of all. If he weren't holding the violin, he could possibly touch his toes. Dalley's is not as deep as Steinhardt's but is deeper than Tree's, which is sometimes more of a nicely informal, friendly nod. And when they have a guest artist, they usher him or her off after the piece with back pats or an arm across the shoulder. When the piece is as difficult as the Brahms A Major Quartet, as with Dichter, they step aside, as if to indicate that he deserves special applause.

The Wednesday and Thursday audiences for "Guarneri & Friends" were treated to a typically rich evening: an exhilarating Haydn; the Mozart, finely honed yet spontaneous nevertheless; and the majestic Brahms. And on Friday, the Grace Rainey Rogers stage seats were filled; the maximum number of standees allowed were there; and a large number of people who came to the hall in the hopes of getting a ticket that had been turned in were disappointed. At no time did Soyer play as if he didn't feel well, though after each concert he went directly home and to bed. On all three evenings, the applause was thunderous but brief: two bows, and the audiences rushed for the exits. A disappointment, after Europe. But one aficionado called the Thursday-evening concert one of the great musical experiences of his life.

At Soyer's doctor's orders, the concerts on Long Island, on Saturday, and in Maryland, on Sunday, were canceled, but on the following Thursday, the fourteenth, with Soyer recovered, they left for a tour that would take them to New Orleans, Colorado Springs, Aspen, Salt Lake City, Vancouver, Portland and Corvallis, Oregon, and Palo Alto.

PART V

On April 15, the quartet was once more invited to play at the White House, for a state dinner to honor Menachem Begin, and this time they were free to accept. And for the first time since Bermuda, their wives went along. They were asked to provide thirty minutes of music, and they chose the Dvořák "American" Quartet. At first, they were told they would be seated at dinner in a room off the State Dining Room. It seemed to them that it was an insult, back to the days of Mozart eating with the servants. (One musician friend of theirs, a member of a chamber orchestra, reported to them that before a performance at the White House she had been fed in the basement.) Initially, they decided to eat dinner in the hotel the White House was putting them up in, the Hay-Adams; go to the White House just long enough to play; and then leave. Instead, they sent word through Beall to Gretchen Poston, the social director at the White House, that if they were not seated in the State Dining Room they would not play. Miss Poston told Beall it was a misunderstanding—of course they would sit in the State Dining Room.

At five in the afternoon, on the day of the dinner, Miss Poston, who makes a point of giving performers a chance to gauge the acoustics, scheduled a "sound test" in the East Room. Not reckoning with the quartet, she said the test would take only five minutes. They were picked up at their hotel by a White House minibus and driven to the East Gate. Steinhardt says that at least a thousand times a year someone says to him, "What have you got in there, a machine gun?" and he was surprised that their instrument cases weren't inspected, but then the guard at the gate smiled at him and said, "Where's Dorothea?"

Except for a raised platform, carpeted and holding four chairs and four music stands, against the north wall, the East Room was empty. The vast floor outgleamed the instruments the men took from their cases. Miss Poston, in a tailored tan suit that, together with her efficient manner, suggested she might once have been a stewardess, told them that the press —TV and newspapermen with flash cameras—would be in the room at the beginning of the program. She asked how long the first piece lasted. Steinhardt said, "A little over six minutes," and Soyer said, "It's four movements, but it shouldn't be broken up—interrupted. It's a whole thing." Miss Poston said, "I'd better get Faith Collins up here. She's in charge of the press." She sent an assistant, Marilyn Funderberg, off to call Miss Collins. While the men were waiting, Soyer reached in his pocket—perhaps for a cigarette—and came up with three ticket stubs. He said, "If this jacket is telling the truth, I've been to Philadelphia three times this month." They tuned and began to play the first movement. Miss Collins, in a striped dress and also with an efficient manner, arrived, and she stood in the doorway, listening. The men finished the first movement, and stood when she came up. "Sit down," she said. "You're great. The press will only want a few pictures. Do you want me to usher them out after the President introduces you and before you start to play?" Soyer said, "That makes sense." Miss Collins asked if they wanted their instruments to be out on their chairs when they finished eating, and there was a chorus of "No!"'s. Tree said, "We like to carry them in ourselves. Otherwise we won't know what to do with our hands," which made Dalley grin. Miss Collins added that most "entertainers" skipped dessert and left the dining room to get ready. Tree said, "But that's the best *part!*" and Steinhardt said, "After *two* desserts, we'll warm up."

They were, for them, dressed up—jackets and ties, though Steinhardt's jacket was corduroy. The platform was edged in banks of yellow tulips and lining the rear were stands of cherry blossoms, which Dalley twice, by accident, whacked with his bow. On either side were the huge Gilbert Stuart portraits of George and Martha Washington. Behind the quartet was a gold brocade floor-to-ceiling drape that matched the drapes at the windows. A janitor brought in a ladder and changed bulbs in the candelabra mounted on three of the walls. Three gigantic chandeliers, each with hundreds of lights of various sizes, had presumably already been checked.

The quartet began to rehearse in earnest: "That ritard isn't two before M, it's three before." "When I have that phrase, I wish you'd give me a little time. It's beautiful and you shouldn't *pounce* on me like that." "When did you decide to do that up bow?" "It should be *very* soft before L—a whisper." While they were rehearsing, Heindrik Hertzberg and his father, Sydney, came in to listen. Miss Funderberg, who had lingered to listen, said, "I'd like you to meet the President's No. 1 speechwriter, Rick Hertzberg." The four stood and shook hands with Hertzberg; Soyer almost lifted him off his feet. Hertzberg brought two chairs in from the reception room—where music stands and chairs had been set up for the Marine Orchestra, which would play during dinner—and he and his father sat down and listened. The nitpicking seemed, even for the Guarneri, a lot. Tree used his pencil a couple of dozen times and, looking a little baffled, said, "Did we *record* this?" Dalley said they had. At ten after six, they finished. Hertzberg and his father were going out the door when Soyer said, "Stop! I know you! We've met, but I can't remember where," to Sydney Hertzberg, who smiled and said that they hadn't met before. Dalley looked around the East Room and then at the floor. He said, "I assume someone's going to clean this floor before tonight." Miss Funderberg looked startled, and then she laughed. Walking toward the door, she said, "You'll be picked up in less than half an hour. Don't you want to leave your instruments here?" Steinhardt said, "It's not that easy. We've been carrying them for so long, they can only be removed surgically." Sixteen hundred Pennsylvania Avenue has double glass doors—a protection against inclement weather—and Dalley said, "Where'd they get these doors? It looks like a Ramada Inn." At the door, Miss Funderberg handed them their invitations for the evening.

At the dinner that night, President Carter spoke briefly, and then Prime Minister Begin spoke, at length. The first edition of the Washington *Post,* the next morning, said he "rambled. At times attempting humor, other times pathos." Jani Tree, gazing at all the presidential portraits, didn't mind. She was overwhelmed at what the White House stood for: "Two hundred years of democracy. *Not* a feudal state. Looking at all the presidential portraits, I had such a sense of history, of freedom, knowing that democracy really works. And in no other country is that true." The Trees were sitting with, among others, Mrs. Mondale and the wife of one of the Iranian hostages. The "entertainment," scheduled to start at nine-thirty, began at eleven-fifteen. The East Room had been filled with chairs, except for an aisle to the left for the musicians. Standing outside the East Room door, holding their instruments, they waited for the President to introduce them.

Miss Funderberg appeared and asked them, "How was the dessert?" Steinhardt said, "We didn't get any." Inside, the lights were dimmed as guests and the press took their seats. Suddenly there was a blaze of lights and the President was standing in front of the platform. He said, "I told Mr. Begin that he and I could make beautiful music together. The last time we had dinner together, we heard Itzhak Perlman and Pinchas Zukerman, and Mr. Begin told me, in advance, that they were the greatest." The President laughed, and added, "I chose not to argue with him. Tonight I'm offering Mr. Begin something that *I* call the greatest, and I don't think he'll argue with me." He spoke at some length of the growth of chamber music in America, the new abundance of quartets, and in some detail about the many ways in which the Guarneri was unique. In conclusion, he said, "A Beethoven recording of theirs is on Voyager II, launched in August of 1977, and tonight it is somewhere between Jupiter and Saturn. After it passes Saturn it will go into interstellar space. . . . Ten million years from now, if it's recovered by some remote galactic body, the Guarneri Quartet will still be making beautiful music, as they will for us tonight.

"They are performing for us just one major piece and that is the Dvořák number. He came here, as you know, in 1892. He was a Bohemian. He went to a little place called Spillville, Iowa. And he located there because there was a fairly substantial Bohemian community. He played the organ in the local church. He liked music, and not only that but dancing and the food. And while he was there he was able to listen to a lot of American performers. One of those performing groups was a group of Iroquois Indians who came and put on a musical drama, and from that Dvořák derived several pieces of music —the most famous of which is the one that they will perform tonight. It doesn't have the same rhythm as Indian music, but the style and the mood and the emotion of it will be apparent to all of you.

"It's a great pleasure that I have tonight to introduce to you the Guarneri String Quartet—I think the finest in the world—playing Dvořák's wonderful piece the 'American' Quartet."

The audience applauded, the President sat down in the front row, and the quartet entered. Tree later said he wasn't nervous. The dinner had taken so long that by the time he played, he felt as if he were at home. Soyer, who had played countless times on the White House lawn during his stint with the Navy Band, but had never before been inside, was relaxed, and so was Dalley, as always. Steinhardt, however, who said he hadn't anticipated any special feelings, had a sudden spasm of nerves about playing there. "I had such a feeling of history—past history, ongoing history. And these two men were fighting for their political lives!" Even in their dark suits—the required dress for the evening—Beall would have seen them as "four handsome devils," and they played with tremendous energy and excitement the lushly beautiful quartet, which gives all of them, a number of times, showcase solos that display their great talent and the beauty of the instruments they play. The audience gauchely and wonderfully applauded between movements. Most American audiences, no matter how good a concert is, seem reluctant to show their pleasure. If people stand, chances are it's a prelude to a fast exit. This night, when the quartet finished, the audience leaped to its feet and applauded thunderously. The President, precluding an encore—it had been a long night—stood and shook hands with each man. Then he turned to Begin and the audience and, with a broad smile, said, "Aren't they the greatest?"

150

Guarneri Quartet Recordings

	ALBUM NO.	RCA STEREO R8S-	CASS. RK-
Bartok: The Six String Quartets	ARL3-2412		
Beethoven: The Complete String Quartets and the Grosse Fuge	VCS-11-100		
Beethoven: The Six Early Quartets, Op. 18	VCS-6195		
Beethoven: The Five Middle Quartets: Op. 59, Nos. 1–3 ("Rasumovsky"); Op. 74 ("Harp"); Op. 95	VCS-6415		
Beethoven: The Five Late Quartets; The Grosse Fuge	VCS-6418		
Beethoven: Quintet in C, Op. 29; Mendelssohn: Quintet in B-Flat, Op. 87 Zukerman, Violinist	ARL1-3354		ARK1-3354
Brahms: The Three Piano Quartets, Opp. 25, 26, and 60; Schumann: Piano Quintet in E-Flat, Op. 44 Rubinstein, Pianist	LSC-6188		
Brahms: Quintet in F Minor, Op. 34 Rubinstein, Pianist	LSC-2971		
Debussy/Ravel Quartets	ARL1-0187		
Dvořák: Quartet No. 6 in F, Op. 96 ("American"); Quintet No. 3 in E-Flat, Op. 97 Trampler, Violist	ARL-1-1791	ARS1-1791	ARK1-1791

	RCA		
	ALBUM NO.	STEREO R8S-	CASS. RK-
Dvořák: Piano Quintet in A, Op. 81 Rubinstein, Pianist	LSC-3252		
Fauré: Piano Quartet in C Minor, Op. 15 Rubinstein, Pianist; String Quartet, Op. 121	ARL1-0761		
Haydn: Quartet in D, Op. 20, No. 4; Quartet in G Minor, Op. 74, No. 3	ARL1-3485		ARK1-3485
Haydn: String Quartets, Op. 77	ARL1-2791		ARK1-2791
Mozart: Six Quartets Dedicated to Haydn	CRL-3-1988		
Mozart: Six Quartets Dedicated to Haydn, Vol. 3	ARL1-1153	ARS1-1153	ARK1-1153
Mozart: The Piano Quartets Rubinstein, Pianist	ARL1-2676	ARS1-2676	ARK1-2676
Schubert: Quartet No. 14 in D Minor ("Death and the Maiden"); Wolf: Italian Serenade	ARL1-1994	ARS1-1994	ARK1-1994
Schubert: Quartet No. 15 in G, D.887	ARL1-3003		
Schubert: Quintet in C, Op. 163 Rose, Cellist	ARL1-1154	ARS1-1154	ARK1-1154
Tchaikovsky: Sextet in D Minor, Op. 70 ("Souvenir de Florence") Kroyt, Violist; M. Schneider, Cellist (Previously released as LSC-2916)	ARL1-2286	ARS1-2286	ARK1-2286